FAT AND FAITHFUL

FAT AND FAITHFUL

LEARNING TO LOVE OUR BODIES, OUR NEIGHBORS, AND OURSELVES

J. NICOLE MORGAN

FORTRESS PRESS

MINNEAPOLIS

FAT AND FAITHFUL

Learning to Love Our Bodies, Our Neighbors, and Ourselves

Copyright © 2018 Fortress Press. All rights reserved. Except for brief quotations in critical articles or reviews, no part of this book may be reproduced in any manner without prior written permission from the publisher. Email copyright@1517.media or write to Permissions, Fortress Press, PO Box 1209, Minneapolis, MN 55440-1209.

Cover design: Paul Soupiset

Print ISBN: 978-1-5064-2522-1

eBook ISBN: 978-1-5064-4828-2

The paper used in this publication meets the minimum requirements of American National Standard for Information Sciences — Permanence of Paper for Printed Library Materials, ANSI Z329.48-1984.

Manufactured in the U.S.A.

To Everett, Mia, Natalie, and Brielle.
May you live a life of vibrant, enormous love
in a world that so often tells us to shrink.
It is my great joy to be your aunt.

My frame was not hidden from you
when I was made in the secret place,
when I was woven together in the depths
of the earth.

—Psalm 139:15 (NIV)

The curves of your hips are like jewels,
The work of the hands of an artist.

—Song of Songs 7:1 (NASB)

CONTENTS

INTRODUCTION

I grew up fat and loving Jesus. As one of those kids who was patient and optimistic by nature, I found that faith came easily to me. I don't remember a time when I didn't know about God and feel a love for God. My mother tells me that when I was three years old, I stopped midstride as I was walking out of the living room and nonchalantly announced that I was going to be a missionary when I grew up. As I got older, I genuinely enjoyed living my faith in all the usual ways: church attendance, prayer, Bible reading.

Yet I was frequently distracted and burdened by what I saw as my biggest spiritual and personal flaw: my weight. I was fat. I am fat. That has never changed. I now see the image of God reflected in my body, marveling at the way my size reveals parts of the heart and character of God—contributing to the full body of Christ that is the church. That was not always the case.

I used to flip through my baby book as a young

teenager, scrutinizing the pictures to see when I became fat. I do not remember ever not being fat, but surely it started somewhere. Around four is when the double chin started to show. In one picture around that age, I stood next to my brothers at Disney World—grinning wildly at the joy of it all, my round belly prominent under my shirt that was raised just a bit above my waist. By third grade, there was no question: I was fat. That was the year I found my school picture ripped in half on the floor of the school bus as I exited one afternoon. The only person on the bus who would've had it was my best friend, who lived a few doors down. I picked up the pieces of the picture—my chubby face and unfortunate bangs on one half, my bare arms and the top of my gray dress that I thought looked so grown-up on the other. That's the first time I remember thinking there must have been something wrong with how I looked; why else would my image be ripped in half by someone who was my friend? I remained friends with the girl who I was sure had ripped up my photo until she moved away in middle school. I never told her about finding the picture.

Once, when I had been absent from school for a few days, I returned to my classmates joking that they thought maybe I couldn't fit through the door anymore. Another time, someone called me fat as I walked down the school hallway, and my friend, the one who had torn my picture up, turned around and responded with a fierce protectiveness. At home, I was not chastised for my weight. My mother did at times lament her own figure and would occasionally tell me she wanted better for me.

From an early age, I heard fatness mentioned as a sin from the pulpit. I eventually grew to hate my body and believed with passionate conviction that not only was my body wrong and ugly, it was ungodly. I fully believed that my body was shameful and an embarrassment to God. I believed that I had wasted the gift of my body, my temple, and could offer nothing of worth. I believed that everything I had was tainted and unusable because it all came from a body that was fat and therefore sinful.

At the age of fifteen, I wrote in my diary that I wanted to lose one hundred pounds in the next year. I wrote out my prayer: "God, I will try my best to lose weight, because my body is your temple and deserves to be treated with care. Please God help me to resist temptations, and if it's your will to meet my goal." The next year I wrote, "I am not where God wants me. I am not in His best will for me. Mainly because I abuse his temple—my body. It is supposed to be a holy and righteous act of worship to him, and it is not. It is a temple of worship to food and gluttony.

SIN. I say I love God and would do anything for him, but do I really?"

I wrote my plans in my journal. Diets, exercise, accountability, prayers, Scripture memorization —no matter what I did or what I tried, I couldn't become thin. I was convinced that my weight was a walking billboard telling the world that I didn't really love God. I reasoned that if I loved God, if I believed in Jesus, then I would have the Holy Spirit, and by extension the fruit of the spirit. I would have love, joy, peace, patience, and self-control. And if my wide hips said anything, they shouted that I lacked self-control. Everyone knew that if you just ate less and moved more, you would be thin. But all I could tell myself when I looked in the mirror as a teenager was that I clearly loved something else more than God. Even worse, I feared that I would give God a bad name. I didn't think I could tell anyone that God can change things and make all things new when God couldn't even transform me.

After I graduated high school, I decided to spend my entire summer helping a church in a small mountain town in the Appalachian hills of West Virginia. I worked alongside six other high-school- and college-age interns and the two pastors at the local church. We organized food and clothing giveaways, ran day camps for kids, cleaned up the church to make the space functional, and loved and served the local community who called the Appalachian town home.

The Sunday before I left, I sat on the pew of my home church, next to the other girl who would be serving with me, and I was overwhelmed with guilt. I could not imagine why God would allow me the opportunity to serve in such a visible way when I had failed to discipline my body into thinness. I grabbed the hand of my friend and asked her to pray with me at the altar. She did—agreeing with me that God is good to use us despite our flaws. We praised God's mercy at using those of us like me whose sin hangs in swaying drapes off the back of our arms for all the world to see. As we knelt at the altar, hot tears fell silently down my cheeks. I was so ashamed that I was heading into a summer of working for a church in a fat body. I was so ashamed that I was supposed to spend my summer telling people about the power of God and the importance of serving God while my very presence would be a hindrance to that message. God could not narrow my waist, but I was about to spend a summer telling people that God could transform the world. I believed I had no credibility to tell people to surrender their life when every jiggle of my arm sent out a signal that my life was ruled by laziness and gluttony.

I felt completely undeserving of the chance to serve when I felt so deeply flawed. I was humbled by the grace of God to allow my sinful body to serve. The confession at the altar was my acknowledgment that I was trying to be good and thin; I firmly believed that my body was wrong. I remained racked with guilt, but I went anyway.

If you have thought similar thoughts, please know that they are lies. I have learned over time to see these lies, identify them, and push back. Sometimes that has meant seeing a fat joke from a popular Christian author online and just naming it quietly to myself. Sometimes it has meant responding to articles rooted in fat shame and specifically responding to the way fat bodies are marginalized. Sometimes I will point out problematic analogies and illustrations to those I hope will truly be able to hear my critique. Embracing my fat body and all it has to offer has given me peace and joy that I can share with others. You are qualified to love and serve God, no matter your body. God delights when people of all shapes and sizes love and serve their neighbors. I pray this book makes that truth known in the deep parts of your soul.

A few weeks into the summer I interned in West Virginia, we spent a day sorting and organizing the clothes donated to the church clothes closet. Later that day, we met back in the office for our standard meeting. Some of the other interns had found a pair of women's underwear and stretched it across the boxy computer monitor in the office. They all got a good laugh at how large those panties were. They couldn't imagine how big someone must be to need the underwear that stretched easily over the monitor. I laughed along uncomfortably. The panties would fit me, maybe. They might have been too small. As a fat person, I have a body that is simultaneously highly visible and yet invisible. My coworkers, brothers and sisters in the body of Christ, were mocking a body that was standing in front of them, and they didn't even know it. I tried to hide my shame. I hoped somehow it was a sign they did not know that the joke-inducing undergarments would fit me. That God's grace was covering my flaws in order for his name to be made great in spite of my fat body. It seemed my back rolls did not speak louder than my love for God.

My heart breaks for my eighteen-year-old self and for all who silently endure shame when fellow Christians speak and act in ignorance. My prayer is that I speak up in such situations—whether the bodies and lives being mocked are fat people, immigrants, people of color, women, persons with disabilities, or any number of people who receive ridicule.

I do believe that my coworkers would not have laughed if they had known the shame it brought, if they had heard someone they knew and trusted speak up and offer correction.

I believed I was a fat person with a thin person inside, trying to get out, and the thin person tried to be on her best behavior. As a Christian, that meant that I needed to discipline my body until it became godly and thin.

It would be five years after my summer in West Virginia before I would first read the phrase *fat acceptance*. I stumbled upon it while I was trying desperately to find fashion tips that would make me look slimmer. I was a junior in college and had my first boyfriend. The fact that he started dating me as a fat girl did nothing to convince me that he wouldn't want me thinner. Years of trying to be thinner had proved unsuccessful, but I thought perhaps I would be able to find clothing tricks to at least look a little thinner, a little better. What I found instead was an online community of mostly women who believed that their fat bodies were not wrong. They did not try to hide their fat; they embraced it and treated it as worthy of love and respect. It was a community devoted to plus-size fashion with a side of fat politics and activism. I learned about the structural oppression that fat people face in everything from finding employment to getting adequate health care. I read medical studies that made me question what had been my commonsense understanding: that fat is bad for the body. I learned to call myself *fat* as a way to reclaim a word that is so often used as an insult.

I use the word *fat* specifically and intentionally throughout this book. Fat is an adjective. It speaks to the amount of flesh on a person's body. From a social/political context, this self-naming as *fat* is about destigmatizing fat bodies and pushing back on the way fat bodies are treated. I reject terms such as *overweight* because the word contains an inherent judgment that there is a correct weight. Euphemisms that seek to be positive often set further dichotomies; for example, *curvy* speaks to a male gaze that sexualizes and fetishizes women while still failing to encompass all the curves a body might possess. Other terms, including *fluffy* and *plump*, are the preferred terms of many fat people, but not for me personally. This book will use the word *fat* frequently to both describe myself and others.

I also want to note that there is an important difference between *feeling* fat and *being* fat. Thin persons should not call themselves fat in an effort to be allies to fat people. The way an individual person feels about their body is important and significant, but the way others perceive a fat body contributes to various oppressions that will be addressed throughout the book. If you are not sure if you feel fat or if you are fat, think about whether or not your body prevents your access to spaces or things because of its size. Consider whether you have trouble finding seating or clothing, or if you regularly check weight limits on things and find that your body exceeds the limits. Regardless of whether you are fat or not, there is much to learn about how our world, our churches, and our communities interact with fat people.

As I've come to understand the social and political implications of fat acceptance and to see the oppression and discrimination where it exists, I've become increasingly passionate about challenging any body-type prioritization and pointing out its flaws—both in terms of anti-fatness and in regards to racism and other oppression. *Intersectionality* says people can experience oppression and discrimination for more than one reason. My freedom to live in a fat body is bound up in the freedom of all others to live without fear in their bodies. The humanity and freedom of fat people is bound up in the humanity and freedom of all. Loving my neighbor as my fat self means that I work for justice both for people who face oppression as a result of their fat body and for those who also endure the judgment and systematic oppression that comes with other marginalized identities.

Four years after I first heard about fat acceptance, I found myself kneeling at the altar of my church once again. I was not praying about my body that time. A woman I had known for years came over to me, placed her hand on my shoulder, and began to pray over me out loud. "Dear God," she said, "please help Nicole to overcome her sin of being overweight. I know how hard it is to walk around where all the world can see your sin." All this woman saw was my fatness. She was also fat, and I imagine she thought she understood what drove me to the altar; perhaps her own body shame fueled most of her prayers. I have no doubt she was trying to show empathy and solidarity. All I heard, though, was that all that mattered was my body. I knew better this time.

Four years into learning about fat acceptance, this moment sparked a fire. Later I would realize it was this moment that began my journey toward a calling to tell others that their fat bodies are okay. I knew my message would specifically be about how Christians talk about bodies. God cares about our broken hearts, not the wideness of our calves. I stubbornly choose to believe that God is about restoring broken things: broken dreams, broken hearts, and especially broken theologies that hurt rather than heal. Any theology that sees first the size of someone's hips cannot be the message of a God who showed up on earth and taught us to love our neighbors as ourselves.

My struggle with my body image and how my body fits into the body of Christ is not unique. I've spent the past decade speaking to friends and strangers about my experience with Christian fat shame. I hear similar stories over and over—people who tell me that they believed there was something spiritually wrong with them because they were fat, that it disqualified them from serving God, or that they were afraid that they were giving God a bad name. Thin Christians have expressed similar spiritual fears to me about becoming fat.

It is not a struggle unique to our modern times. Though the modern Christian weight-loss message and industry arguably began with the 1957 publication of Charlie Shedd's *Pray Your Weight Away*, we as Christians have a long history of not knowing what to do with our bodies in relationship to God and our spiritual life. The religious of Jesus's day created numerous rules about whose body was acceptable or not; Jesus rejected those classifications and touched the untouchable. Our Christian heritage is filled with stories of people of faith who believed that intentionally inflicted physical pain and suffering brought them (or others) closer to God. Gnostic beliefs that devalue the body entirely, finding it a stumbling block to a pure faith, have crept into the theologies of Christianity.

In the name of seeking purity and holiness, Christians have frequently decided that our bodies deserve scorn or punishment. This is a lie. I hope that by the end of this book, you will be able to see the ways that lies weave their way into well-intentioned talks about our bodies, holiness, and spiritual disciplines. I hope you will be able to call these lies out, first to yourself and then to others, and instead live victoriously in the body you have right now.

God is not ashamed of you.

God is not ashamed of your body.

Our right to speak is not taken away by our imperfect bodies.

A body the world calls flawed does not invalidate the wonder and power of our Creator.

No one's size, appearance, or ability prohibits that person from serving neighbors with love.

My prayer for this book, and for you as you read it, is that you find in these pages reason to question the narrative that fat bodies are not good enough for God. Learning to combat the body-shaming lies we were raised in is a multiyear journey for most of us; I hope this book is part of that journey for you.

1

MADE IN THE IMAGE OF GOD

I stood in front of the vanity mirror in my bedroom and smiled at my adolescent reflection, finding beauty reflected in the glass of the antique heirloom furniture that my great-grandmother once used. I liked my eyes the most, and my smile too. Sometimes, on rare occasions, I thought perhaps I was even pretty. My smile abruptly turned into a stern look that wrinkled my forehead. "Stop it!" I whispered fiercely to my reflection, eager to correct the train of my thoughts. I held up my arm and pushed at the flab that hung low, then grabbed the soft drape of my stomach and scowled. "Snap out of it, Nicole. What you're seeing is a lie. This is not okay. You're being deceived into not doing anything about this problem in your life." I told myself that this belief that I was appealing had to be a lie designed to destroy my motivation and ability to lose weight as God would want me to do.

"God doesn't want you fat. So fat can't be beautiful, no matter what you see in the mirror." That was my mantra through middle school and high school; the scene in front of the mirror repeated itself many times. I told myself, and never anyone else, that I had reverse anorexia. Anorexics, I heard, looked in the mirror and saw fat. I looked in the mirror and saw pretty. We both, I firmly believed, saw lies. In my mind, beauty and fat were opposites. They could not exist together simultaneously. My ability to see beauty instead of fat had to be a distorted perception, because I firmly believed that as a Christian, I should care for my body as the temple of God and honor it by getting skinny. Liking the body I saw in the mirror was only a distraction from that goal.

My young heart knew the truth: I was beautiful. Sadly, that truth was drowned out and overcome by the message I heard everywhere else.

In a sense, I was the victim of my own internal gaslighting, in which every good thing I believed about myself was instead used as a weapon to prove my unworthiness of love or respect. My vision was so distorted by these lies that I would pick up the Bible and read, "You are wonderfully made" (Psalm

139:14) and could not believe that the verses were about me. Or I believed that I had somehow ruined my wonderfully made body. I believed it was a lie when I saw myself as beautiful. But the real lie was that I had to do anything to make my body holy and acceptable to God. God had already done that for each and every human body, fat ones included, from the moment of creation.

The Christian concept of embodiment, that our bodies are important to our faith, finds its scriptural origin in the first chapters of Genesis, in which God creates humans in God's own image. In Genesis, we read that on the sixth day of creation, "God created man in his own image, in the image of God he created him, male and female he created them" (Genesis 1:27, ESV). God creates humans in God's own likeness (*imago Dei*) and breathes life into them (Genesis 2:7).

From Genesis to eternal life, our bodies play a prominent role in the work that God does on earth. We are made of dust and breath and bone. We arrive into this world bathed in mess and pain and cries—welcomed or shunned from our first breath because of circumstances outside of our control. Our bodies' existence on this earth as good or bothersome is up for debate and judgment by others from the first moment that our presence is known, yet none of that judgment comes from God.

No matter the shape of our bodies, we are still knit together, wonderfully made, in the image of a vibrant and loving God (Psalm 139). Despite our fears and hopes, and despite the cultural expectations about our bodies, the truth is that our bodies are made in the image of God and loved as holy and acceptable from our first moment of being. My favorite part of Psalm 139 is verse 15. Many translations say, "My frame was not hidden from you." The King James Version says, "My substance was not hidden from you." The original Hebrew word translated as "frame" or "substance" is transliterated as *otsem*, which means "power, bones, might, . . . strong, substance." The outline of my body, the way the bones and muscles and substance come together to take up more space than many others, was not hidden from God in the earliest days of my creation. My power and strength and the *substance* of who I am were not hidden from God, did not come as a shock to God. There was no rush to figure out a quick plan B on my purpose as my stomach rounded from even a young age.

There is much talk of beauty and bodies in Scripture. Rachel is lovely. Saul is handsome. But not all bodies of worth are given descriptors of beauty.

Visual appeal is not a requirement for image bearers of God. In Isaiah, we read the prophecy that the Messiah would have "no beauty or majesty to attract us to him, nothing in his appearance that we should desire him" (Isaiah 53:2, NIV). There is room to critique what is beautiful or not (and we'll talk about beauty in chapter eight), but not every body will be aesthetically appealing. That does not change the worth of that person one bit. In our culture, fatness is not often associated with beauty, though that is changing a bit with contemporary fat-positive and body-positive movements. Whether or not someone finds a fat person beautiful, even if that someone is the fat person in question, has absolutely nothing to do with the worth of that person or whether that person is made in the image of God. God's image is not always beautiful; it is always good and worthy of love and dignity.

When God incarnate shows up on this earth, it is in the form of a human body. We—full of breath and bones—are ever-present pictures of the physical reality of our Messiah. Jesus came to earth, put elbows on tables, and felt the heat of sun on his brow. When we disconnect from our bodies because we loathe them, we miss the chance to connect with the way Jesus understands and experienced our human existence. When we disconnect from our bodies because all we want is for them to be less, to be unnoticeable, we disconnect from the reality that Jesus felt pain, enjoyed water and wine, and walked dusty roads in pursuit of his calling. The danger of forgetting that these are things Jesus experienced is that we also forget they are things that make us human. We are on this earth to live fully, to make present the kingdom of God on earth as it is in heaven. God frequently invites us into that experience by inviting us to live in our body here on earth: eat, drink, dance, weep. Attempts to subdue our body limit our ability to fully live our life. If we ignore our own physical realities of pain or joy, we are more likely to ignore others' pain and joy. That inhibits our ability to love neighbors and, especially, enemies.

Our complicated relationship with our body starts early. After Adam and Eve eat the fruit of the tree of the knowledge of good and evil, Genesis 3:7 tells us, "the eyes of both of them were opened, and they realized they were naked; so they sewed fig leaves together and made coverings for themselves" (NIV). Immediately after their first break with the rules that God has set up, they become aware of their bodies in a way that brings shame. They are creatures in a world full of other creatures—covered with skin or fur or feathers, but none with extra clothing, as far as we know. Once sin has entered into the equation, so does shame. And that shame is not about their actions but about their bodies. Most translations indicate that the coverings were for their loins, their genitals—the parts of our body that are used to come together to create more life.

This sin of bodily shame disrupts community. God makes "garments of skin" for Adam and Eve (Genesis 3:21). In a created world that was free of bloodshed and death, the first death is of a nonhuman creature, and it comes to cover the shame of human bodies. Body shame has an impact not only on Adam and Eve's own understanding of who they are and how they interact with God and each other, but also on the rest of their community and all of creation. The word in verse 21 for "garment" indicates a long robe-like garment that covers much more of the body than the small loincloths Adam and Eve made from the fig leaves. The creation of God's skin-garment that covered so much more of the body comes after God tells Eve that her pain in childbirth will be multiplied and tells Adam that he will work and toil under much pain for the ground to produce what had been plentifully abundant before.

This is part of the reality of our world: our bodies will know pain and struggle even in the midst of birthing life and harvesting food. We will cover our bodies, or others will dictate how we cover them, for reasons rooted in shame. But this is not how we are created. Part of our struggle is to get back from Genesis 3 to Genesis 1, to the knowledge that we are created in the image of God and can live free from shame when we live in the freedom of God's plan for abundant life.

This is not to say that a life that rejects body shame becomes one free of pain or toil (or that the best course of action is for everyone to become a nudist). Our world is far too complex, sin too prevalent, for such a simple fix. I am not trying to argue that ending body shame will usher us into an Edenic world. However, every step we can take toward the will of God to come on earth as it is in heaven is a step toward the original goal of creation.

Body shame is one aspect of ways that we are prone to believe we are not enough for God. This shame hinders us from fully living into our calling to be followers of Jesus Christ. Right there in the greatest commandment, we are told that we are to love others as we love ourselves. This is not an egocentric self-love that prioritizes our needs above all others, but a reminder that we have to love ourselves in order to love our neighbors. Think of it as the original version of the airlines' rules to put your own oxygen mask on first. Neighbor love is a concept we see from Genesis to Revelation, showing us how to bring the kingdom of God to earth as it is in heaven. If I love my neighbors as I loved my teenage self, I would go around reminding everyone that their virtues mean nothing in comparison to their flaws. That's not very loving or effective for building up the body of Christ and making a better world.

We'll love ourselves more—and, therefore, our neighbors more—if we understand the truth that our bodies are made in the image of God. And we don't have to do anything or change anything to make them worthy of such a distinction. This truth first shows up in Genesis, and it is reinforced in weighty form when Jesus shows up in a body and walks around loving his neighbors—feasting, drinking, washing people's feet, getting accused of gluttony, and hanging out with others whose bodies are deemed unworthy. The many varied parts of the body are all found wonderful and worthy of serving God. Bodies matter, and every body gets to be a part. None is deemed unworthy or incapable of serving God. When Jesus ascends, he leaves behind his church—the body of Christ (a body we will talk about more in the next chapter)—as well as the Holy Spirit, which becomes a part of each Christian's body.

During Jesus's time on earth, he tells his disciples that the Spirit will come "guide [us] into all the truth" (John 16:12, NIV). The New Testament frequently reminds us that the Spirit lives inside each of us who have received that Spirit. We can quench or grieve the Holy Spirit, but the Spirit does not find the body of any believer uninhabitable. There is no scenario in which the skin (or the tissue under it) that covers the body of a believer is too thick for the Spirit to pass through.

We are made in the image of God, we live in a body of flesh just as Jesus himself did, and we live and breathe with the Spirit indwelling our lives and minds and hearts in order to lead us in the truth and love of God. My body tells part of my faith story and proclaims not only that God created, loves, and accepts my fat body, but also that my fat body, has something unique and Godlike to offer to the world. My body is a reflection of the image of God, and that includes my fatness. There is a beauty and a life-giving story in the way my hips spread wide or my chest is always a soft place for someone to lay their head. The way my body is a warm embrace for those who lie in my arms is a picture of what the church should be to those in need of rest or comfort. My body can be immovable—a picture of what calm persistence and dedication can look like. When

I fail to love that quality in myself, I miss the opportunities to encourage that quality in the church or to be a model of what it can look like to be immovable. I miss seeing the beauty of those qualities in my neighbors.

As a child, I grew up next door to two elderly women who were sisters. They were like grandmothers to me; my own grandmothers lived many hours away. Ms. Trudy, the older of the two sisters, would walk over to our house on Sunday mornings and ride with us to church. I was fascinated by the way the skin of her upper arm wobbled. When we sat next to each other in the car, I would push at the back of her arm and make it jiggle. She looked down, returned my delighted smile, and held her arm up a bit so that on my next push, it jiggled even more. Ms. Trudy's delight at the joy of her body is the joy we are to have at the body of Christ. It is the joy we are supposed to have in our bodies. Ms. Trudy's delight did not stop me from scowling at my own arm fat many years later, but her joy stayed with me as another way to view the body. These days, my oldest niece will often cuddle up next to my own fat arm. It's her go-to spot for snuggles. She sits beside me, reaches her small hand around my arm to rest it inside the bend of my elbow, and leans the side of her face into my arm. She'll take a moment to do this while we sit at the table for dinner or will take a break from her play to run up next to me as I sit on the floor. Fat arms are good for children and make visible the love, warmth, and comfort of God.

We have to speak of our bodies in ways that acknowledge they are made in the image of God just as they come. The image of God includes every unique or definite characteristic of bodies that exists. It is biologically natural for bodies to vary in appearance; we see it in all of creation. Depending on the species of creature, there are variations in coloring, size, personality, life span, and more. We accept this easily enough for humans in regards to height or the presence (or lack) of freckles. Western history has been less accepting that various skin tones and hair types are naturally occurring variations of a good creation, but that, too, is true despite popular and flawed teaching.

If grocery stores would sell us all the produce that comes from the ground, instead of just the fruits and vegetables that look like we expect them to look, we would see creation's diversity on our weekly strolls through the produce department. Carrots are not always long, thin, and orange. We have just learned to expect them that way, so farmers breed them to grow homogeneously and then send the ones that grow in other shapes to sellers who will use them to make alternative products. Grocers then sell neat little bundles that appeal to our sense of order and control. This is not the world God created, though. Variety is inherent in creation. We are not made wonderfully in the image of God in spite of what we see as flaws and deviations, but rather, those are the things that most accurately reflect the image of God when viewed as parts of a whole. God is not always conventionally attractive. God does not always look like our definition of right or good.

If each individual person is made in the image of God, then our own unique image must be part of the whole picture of God. God's image is not and cannot be only thin, because I exist. God is not white, because the world is not entirely white. God is not male, because there is not a single gender on this planet that has exclusively received the breath and Spirit of God. God is bigger than a single human form. We each reflect part of God's image. When we deny that truth and fail to discover what God has to teach us—that God's image on earth is expressed in bodies of all shapes, sizes, skin tones, abilities, genders, and giftings—we miss knowing something important about God.

Throughout history, the dominant powers of the world have done a fairly extensive job of telling us a different story. In the United States, white, wealthy, typically abled, straight, cisgender men are given power, and the rest of us have spent too much time trying to reach second place on the backs of each other. Those with perceived mental and physical differences have been locked away in institutions. Black men, women, and children were shackled beneath the decks of ships and enslaved because their bodies were not believed to be made in the image of God. Indigenous people were removed from their land and suffered genocide. Women were forbidden from holding public office, from standing in pulpits, from walking streets alone. LGBTQI people have been forced into devastating physical and mental trauma in the name of making them conform to social norms. People were hidden away or forced into positions that made it clear their bodies were considered to be worth less.

As a result, being visible in the world in our body is an important part of living our embodiment. This is especially true for people who live in what has historically or culturally been called a body of lesser value. Fat people have not faced a systematic and intentional campaign to literally enslave or exterminate us, but the bias against fat bodies is prevalent. (We do endure frequent reminders that much of our culture endorses a war on obesity. They don't want us dead, they say, just thin.) In the not-too-distant past, fat bodies, especially those of fat women, were the objects of mockery and entertainment as literal circus side shows. Today that same understanding of fat bodies shows up in our entertainment, as television shows mock and judge the ways fat people live their lives. We watch these shows not to see the image of God in these fat bodies but to voyeuristically gape in disbelief at what many find grotesque or unfathomable. Fat bodies become either a cautionary tale or altogether invisible.

To live into our embodiment, we must practice being visible in our bodies just as we are. In doing so, we encourage others through example to embrace their embodiment, rather than to believe they need to change their body to make it holy. This can look like being in the picture instead of behind the camera, joining the worship team at church, signing up to teach a class, heading outside to enjoy a sport, or any number of actions we can take to put our fat bodies into a place where we have been scared to be visible. It can be anxiety producing at first, but it gets easier. I have found that courage breeds courage.

We undertake an important theological task when we see and embrace the *imago Dei* in humans of all shapes, sizes, and abilities—starting with our own. Thanks to our cultural and theological conditioning, this requires, at least at first, a deliberate and purposeful decision to reject a narrow view of acceptable body types. In addition, we must live with a sense of our own embodiment. This will look different for each person as we learn to reject body shame and instead live in a way that embraces our embodiment.

Here is the bottom line: your body, just as it is right now, is made in the image of God. We as humans failed to recognize that truth pretty early on, but God kept reminding us. Jesus showed up in this same fragile flesh, and when he left, the Spirit stayed behind and deemed human bodies worthy even still.

As beings made in the image of God, we are gifted and entrusted with the same creative power and loving kindness that characterize God. No human judgment about which bodies are good bodies changes the truth of that. Our calling, whether we are fat or thin, is the same: to love God and to love our neighbors as ourselves. When we actively chose to love ourselves in acknowledgment of the truth that our bodies are worthy and able to fulfill God's calling upon our lives, we are better equipped to go forward to love God, love neighbors, and love even our enemies.

2

THE BODY OF CHRIST

I made a profession of faith at a summer camp when I was sixteen years old. Despite having been in church my entire life and calling myself a Christian, I wasn't sure if I had done the formula right. My faith tradition emphasized being able to name the day and hour of our salvation. I couldn't; I had been three years old when I told my mother that I believed in Jesus. As a teenager, it terrified me that I could not name the day or tell the story. I was not certain I had converted correctly. So at summer camp one year, after years of wondering if I needed to, I chose to walk the aisle and made a profession of faith. I followed in the footsteps of many others at my church who made similar decisions. Looking back now, I don't believe I *needed* that moment to be loved and embraced by God, but after that day, I had a sense of peace that I'd never had before. I'm glad I did it.

After my profession, I wanted to get baptized right then and there, in the pool on the campus of Covenant College in Lookout Mountain, Georgia, where the Student Life camp was happening. My motivation to move quickly had little to do with my newfound enthusiasm for faith. I was anxious because I feared there would not be a baptismal robe to fit me at the church when we got home. I imagined myself climbing the short set of stairs into the baptismal pool with a white robe stretched tightly over my body, clinging to every roll of fat—a spectacle that would only be emphasized when I came out the other side, skin cold and wet with a newly translucent robe.

But I was too shy and nervous about asking to be baptized at the camp, so I spent the remainder of camp, the bus ride home, and the waiting days until the next Sunday wondering if the robe would even stretch over my body, or if I would be forced to wade into the small pool in shorts and a T-shirt. To make matters worse, I got my period the day before my baptism, and my mother advised I ask the pastor if it was still okay to be baptized under those circumstances. Suffice to say, this sacramental moment, one of the most important for a Christian, was a very awkward day to be in my body.

The youth pastor deferred my menstruation question to a female youth leader, and I was set to wade into the waters. Thankfully, my church's largest robe was not as tight as I had imagined, though I doubt it would fit my body today. When I graduated high school a couple of years later, our graduation robes were white, and mine was larger than that baptismal robe. After graduation, I donated it to the church and told them to keep it in the baptism dressing rooms just in case someone needed it one day.

Years later, I read an interview with Rick Warren, author of the best-selling Christian weight-loss book *The Daniel Plan*. In the interview, he tells the reporter about his motivation to write the book. The inspiration behind Warren's diet book came while he was "doing baptisms 'the old-fashioned way'—by physically raising and lowering people into the water."[1] Warren said that as he was "lowering people, [he] literally felt the weight of America's obesity problem [and he] thought, 'good night, we're all fat!'"[2] My mind flashed back to my sixteen-year-old self, wading into baptismal waters with jiggly thighs and a snug baptismal robe. Warren used a sacrament that welcomes us as beloved children into the family of God to issue judgment on the very people he pronounced new life over as he lifted them from the water.

As a teenager, I was afraid my baptismal robe wouldn't fit. But more than that, I was afraid of not fitting into life, of being unwelcomed, and what that might mean about my ability to fully participate in the life of the church. My experience in the years since then has taught me that I was not the only one with this fear. Certainly it is a fear that others feel regardless of their body size, but it is a fear that seems almost universal to fat people of faith. This fear hinders people from being a part of the body of Christ, which in turns hinders our ability to fulfill the mission of the church—to love God, love neighbors, and make the kingdom of God known on earth.

When our churches exclude people through fat bias or structural barriers, we can't carry out that mission to our fullest potential. When the people already inside our walls feel too much shame about their bodies to live vibrantly into the calling God has for their lives, we can't extend love to those outside the church. The many layers of shame and bias around fat bodies exclude people from joining or fully participating in the joyful life that God offers.

THE PEOPLE OF GOD

Our calling as the people of God has its roots in the Hebrew Scriptures. There we find a picture of a welcoming people from the very beginning. The people of God, the Israelites, are called, over and over again, to welcome others and to make the name of God great to the ends of the earth through that welcome.

Part of the responsibility of being God's people includes caring for foreigners and those in their own society who lack access to wealth and resources. In a long list of rules and laws in Leviticus, nestled in between a verse about honoring the elderly and being fair in business, are two verses about welcoming the foreigner: "When a foreigner resides among you in your land, do not mistreat them. The foreigner residing among you must be treated as your native-born. Love them as yourself, for you were foreigners in Egypt" (Leviticus 19:33–34, NIV). The emphasis on community and on making sure that people are welcome, no matter what, is reiterated again and again. The elderly do not get tossed out, people who are foreign and new are not excluded, and people with power and wealth do not get to cheat those who must do business with them. One standard after another emphasizes God's heart for community and inclusion.

Take, for example, the story of Ruth. When Ruth travels with her mother-in-law from Moab to Bethlehem, she finds food to harvest that she did not plant, intentionally left on the edges of the field for people in need. Then Ruth and Naomi devise a plan to marry Ruth to Boaz, a man who is Ruth's distant relative and can serve as a kinsman-redeemer for her.

One way the Israelites made sure vulnerable women were cared for was to require male relatives to marry and care for the widows of their brothers. Ruth's experience with the Israelites is one of welcome despite her poverty and her status as a widow. She is welcomed in, just as she is, with resources and systems in place to make sure she can thrive in this new community.

There is no Levitical law that says, "Do not mock or exclude a fat person." But it's there in spirit, if not in letter.

In the New Testament, this radical welcome is emphasized further. Jesus makes his debut in the world in the midst of outcasts: a young woman, visitors to a city, and poor shepherds. Before his childhood is over, Jesus is a refugee taking flight to a foreign country and receiving the gifts of the magi (who practiced a religion other than Judaism). Jesus's life and ministry welcome and love those who are shunned. Jesus shows them that their bodies—the ways these bodies are used, the diseases they might carry, the labor they perform—do not disqualify them from the right to be counted as beloved children of God who have a place in his community.

Among those who were outcast from the community in the first century because of their bodies were women and lepers. Yet throughout the four Gospels, we see that Jesus has no problem engaging with either. In Luke 7, Jesus is invited to dine at the house of Simon the Pharisee—a man who spends much of his life drawing boundaries around who and what is considered acceptable. While Jesus is there, a woman whose body is viewed as sinful by the men at the table kneels at the feet of Jesus and washes his feet with her tears and anoints them with an ointment (Luke 7:36–50).

Imagine the scene. The table is set with food. Jesus, Simon, and the other guests are reclined about the table, eating their meal. The Pharisees are, as always, on the lookout for evidence of the way Jesus disrupts their world and order. They quickly find a reason when a woman enters the home and approaches Jesus. We know from the story that her worth is questionable in the eyes of the guests at the table because "she lived a sinful life" (Luke 7:37,

NIV). However, this woman has seen or felt something to be true about Jesus, and she comes to honor
him with a jar of perfume. She pushes back against
the rules that say her body dictates what she is
allowed to do, the faith she is allowed to express, or
the love she is allowed to share. She washes Jesus's
feet with her tears, dries them with her hair, and
then anoints them with her jar of expensive perfume. Her whole body is engaged in this act of love
and devotion. Her body, in the eyes of many, has
been wasted. It has been misused. The men at the
table believe that she has failed to honor her temple
and can imagine no scenario in which she is worthy
to engage with them, in which she has anything to
offer the family of God or the world. Yet still she
comes with her tears and her long, flowing hair and
her jar of expensive perfume that came into her pos-
session at a cost we will never know. If her body
is wasted as they say it is, then she has nothing to
lose in wasting this perfume, too. She pours out all
her wealth, all she has to offer, in service and praise
of the one who shows her that she is not wasted
after all—that she is not used up or too much. Jesus
accepts her offering and her love; he does not recoil
from her touch.

Simon sneers that Jesus would send her away if
he only knew who was touching him, if he knew

"what kind of woman she is—that she is a sinner" (Luke 7:39, NIV). Jesus does not turn her away. Jesus honors her body, even the parts deemed shameful and sinful. The Pharisees are shocked that Jesus welcomes and accepts a woman whose body is viewed as worthless by the men and leaders around her because it does not meet their standards for purity and respectability. Jesus rejects this narrative by reminding the Pharisees that they, too, are sinners.

The church is full of sinners—thin sinners, fat sinners. We are each called to participate in the life of the church, to welcome the stranger and the outcast to the table. We are each called to offer our lives and bodies up in service to the Creator God in our calling to love God, love neighbors, and love even our enemies. Our bodies, no matter how far out of conventional bounds they are, do not disqualify us from participating in this venture together with the whole body of Christ. To exclude another's body is to mock the grace and inclusive love of Jesus, who honors the gift of tears and ointment from the woman who empties herself to honor him.

I used to be a member of a small church that met in a beautiful sanctuary. Behind the altar was a massive stained-glass window, and the sun shone brilliantly through the blues and purples and grays every Sunday morning, lighting up the large room and the wooden beams across the high arched ceiling. That weekly service included a few moments of traditional liturgy. We said, "Thanks to be God" together after the reading of Scripture, walked forward to dip our piece of Communion bread into a common goblet, and each week sang the doxology and recited the Lord's Prayer in unison. I tried to tune into the individual voices in the congregation as we said the Lord's Prayer. Some weeks, there was a voice that rose above the crowd; other weeks, we seemingly spoke as one. Some weeks, the quiet hiss of an oxygen tank was the most prominent voice, keeping us in rhythm. A preteen boy was a part of the congregation, one of only a few children, and he loved the Lord's Prayer. He would listen intently for the pastor's cue that we were about to begin the prayer. One week, he beat us all to the start and excitedly rushed through the familiar words. There was a bit of confusion, and then the congregation sped up and he slowed down until we all were reciting, in unison, "Thy kingdom come . . . on earth as it is in heaven." This communal prayer as we gathered together as a church each week became one of my favorite spiritual practices—the bodies and unique abilities and personalities of each person making themselves known in those few moments. This is what community looks like: individual voices for a common prayer. We could have chosen to shush the overexcited boy and instruct him on the proper pacing of the prayer. Instead, he was welcomed with all his eagerness and excitement and the lack of polish that came with his youthful exuberance. We did that prayer together, and we all learned to accommodate for the other while we found the pace that worked.

I hear from the world and from the church that my fat body is too much for them. The world tells me that feasting and joy and grand displays are wrong because I've already had enough, that my body is too much and too conspicuous. But Jesus shows up on the scene and doesn't care when the woman who has been told that her body is too much goes for one more extravagant indulgence to thank him for his inclusion and love. She is an integral, needed part of the community of faith.

Throughout Scripture, we hear a message repeated: "Open your doors a little wider. Make more room at the table." When we exclude people, either because we fail to effectively combat the secular norms about what a good body is or because we don't have baptismal robes in a full range of sizes, we damage our ability to fully welcome everyone into the body of Christ.

THE BODY OF CHRIST

When the writers of the New Testament sought to find a way to talk about the people of God as a collective whole, they used a concept we all know well: the body. Paul tells us, "We were all baptized by one Spirit so as to form one body—whether Jews or Gentiles, slave or free—and we were all given the one Spirit to drink" (1 Corinthians 12:13, NIV). Jews and gentiles, those on the lowest rung of the social order and those higher up—we make up one *body*. That one body consists of bodies made in the image of God and, as Paul points out, filled with the Holy Spirit. Just in case the metaphor is not clear, Paul elaborates: we are eyes and ears and feet. "If the whole body were an eye, where would the sense of hearing be?" (1 Corinthians 12:17, NIV). If the whole body were thin, we would never discover the way a fat body offers warmth and strength and stability in unique ways.

This body is a church that lives and thrives despite all her variations (and more than a few imperfections). We are the body of Christ—all of us, all together. We've got thin legs and really wide hips. Just as the message for the people of God in the Old Testament is to welcome the stranger and Jesus's life is all about including the outcast, we, the people of

28

God, are also called to extend welcome. We live out the calling of that inclusive body best when every part is called, equipped, and given the freedom to work. For each part to work, it doesn't need to be the ideal version of that part. That standard of perfectionism creates a narrative of shame that sets up an unattainable standard. Instead, each part of the body is valuable just as it is. Of course, there is room for discipleship and spiritual growth, but we are not required to achieve any certain spiritual skill before we can begin welcoming each person into our community. As a Christian community, we will not fully understand the full beauty of the body of Christ, the image of God, until we include all the voices that make up that body.

This truth is evident from the very beginning of the Gospels, as we read the lineage of Christ. I have heard countless sermons on the people included in that list, on the wonder and beauty that they are imperfect and flawed and include non-Judaic people. An exclusive faith that is only for certain people does not make sense. Either we are all welcome and needed, or the Gospels don't make sense. Rahab, Bathsheba, Tamar, and Ruth add an authenticity and texture to the lineage of Jesus. The woman with the ointment, Zacchaeus the tax collector, Saul the enemy of the church, and me—a fat woman—add depth and variety to the tapestry of the church.

A church made up of a single type of person is not only boring but also unwelcoming. Anyone who does not fit the mold has no reason to attempt to enter into that community. I don't worship a God who sided with the sneering men at the table or worried about his reputation if he associated with a certain type of woman. I worship a God who risks being called a glutton to make sure everyone knows they are equipped and able to worship God just as they are—even with a shunned body. That freedom propels me on to make that same welcome known to others. When I was so busy trying to get my body into a shape that was acceptable to serve, I only had time for myself. When we all look different, when our scars and our flaws and our variations show, we create a more intriguing picture of what community looks like. Those outside have more reason to believe there is a place for them at that table, too.

There are two passages about honoring the temple that are frequently used to tell fat people to slim down. One is in 1 Corinthians 6, and we will discuss the passage in chapter 5. The other is in 1 Corinthians 3. It reads, "You are God's temple and God's spirit dwells in you. If anyone destroys God's temple, God will destroy [them]" (1 Corinthians 3:16–17,

ESV). There is an online translation of the Bible that uses "y'all" where the text speaks in second-person plural. It reads, "Do y'all not know that y'all are God's temple and that God's Spirit lives in y'all? If someone destroys God's temple, God will destroy him. For God's temple is holy, which is what y'all are" (1 Corinthians 3:16–17, yallversion.com). As a girl from Georgia, I love this version. It makes clear that the Scriptures are talking about us as a community, as a body. In other words, Paul is not sitting down with one person, warning them against the dangers of destroying their individual body; he is warning the collective church that they should take care not to destroy the body of Christ, the church. When we attack, marginalize, and shame-into-hiding individual Christians by policing bodies in the name of honoring the temple, we do precisely the opposite of what this verse is instructing us to do. We destroy the temple.

Let's take God's command to not destroy the temple seriously. Let us not destroy the temple through body shame that prevents individual parts of the body from fully participating. Shaming bodies and causing damage to the dignity of bodies is damaging to the body of Christ. If we create disunity among believers by setting up standards of body image that not all can (or should) obtain, we are splitting the

31

body and introducing envy and strife. If our body shame and body ideals focus inward on the ways our own individual bodies fail, then we are setting up a framework that allows us to abuse our own bodies and to treat them with disrespect. Whether we are talking about the way the body of Christ functions together as a community, or talking about the way our own bodies function, body shame creates dysfunctional experiences. The warnings against destroying the temple are strong. Creating division through determining the holiness of our sisters and brothers by the size of their waist is counter to the will and love of God whose image is found in the body of every human being.

FAT BIAS IN CULTURE AND CHURCH

The church should be a leader in the call for justice and an end to systematic and structural discrimination against fat people, yet the church has fueled and affirmed this bias by giving scriptural, religious weight to cultural ideals.

Perhaps the most memorable of the lines my childhood pastor repeated often was, "I exercise and watch what I eat, so that I don't turn out to be one of those fat and lazy preachers." This was his go-to sermon illustration for self-control. I'd squirm in

32

my seat, cross my arms over my chest in an attempt to make myself smaller, and wonder what he must think about me.

Once a year, we had a revival service in which our home church evangelist, who spent most of his year preaching at other churches, would preach for us. The church supported him financially and through prayer. He was a large man. His voice boomed out in an old-fashioned southern drawl, his sermon volume rose and fell in dramatic cadence, and his stomach was large, very large. My pastor, the one afraid of being "fat and lazy," praised this old-time-southern preacher. He seemed to respect the evangelist despite his girth, but I never believed I could be given the same praise. I believed I would need to convert hundreds of people in order to win that kind of acceptance. I would have to go above and beyond.

We are told on screens and magazine pages that if we just try a little harder and eat less, move more, have a little self-control, then we can be thin and healthy and good. The church carries this narrative a bit further. They point out that self-control is a fruit of the Spirit, and those who are Christians will exhibit that fruit if they are truly living in faith.

In a culture that tells us we are fat because we eat too much and move too little, fatness is seen as a direct result of actions. A fat body in this narrative is a sign of unrepentant sin, that one does not truly live fully into the Spirit of God. Some people may even question whether or not a fat person can be a Christian, finding the person's fatness a sign of persistent, unrepentant sin—thus evidence of an unredeemed life.

Our churches should be places that honor the dignity in every person in our pews and our community while actively working against anything that damages unity. The God who commands that you leave the edges of your field for the poor and that you welcome in the immigrant and the outcast is a God of welcome and generosity. Our church should also offer this kind of generous welcome to all people. When we preach that fatness is a sin and advertise weight-loss classes in our churches, we fail to welcome fat people. We tell people they can sit in our sanctuary, but if they want to stay, they had better start working on their body to make it more acceptable. We are the Pharisees giving a side-eye to the woman whose body they found repulsive. It is such an easy thing to avoid with a little intentionality.

Our churches can offer needed health and wellness classes in a weight-neutral setting. We can encourage people to get regular checkups with medical professionals and empower them to resist the anti-fat bias found even there. We can lead community health classes where we educate people on ways they can begin to be active, no matter their size or ability, and then we can check in with them on how they are feeling, if they have more energy or endurance, if they are able to sleep well at night. A Christian gym owner who had read one of my articles and wanted to know how to make his gym more welcoming to fat people once contacted me to ask for my advice. I took a look at his website and noticed that their main marketing strategy was a collection of before-and-after pictures. The before pictures were all fat; the after pictures were thin. I told him that he needed other ways to mark progress and change. His clients could track their continuous active minutes or the amount of weight they lifted or the number of days they showed up and did something active. Those are all marks of progress; those are all ways we grow.

I will speak more about health in chapter 6, but we do not have to ignore talking about the care of our bodies in order to be a fat-positive church. We just need to welcome fat bodies into our church as they are, with no goal of making them thin.

A communal body of God, made up of many people, that is active in the world and honors the embodiment of each person will offer a picture of the triune God—encouraging and building community in ways that influence our world into looking more like the kingdom of God. We all, especially as the church, are called to live in this world together as a reflection of God's self in order to love our neighbors and enemies and welcome the kingdom of God on earth as it is in heaven.

NOTES

1. Alexandra Wolfe, "Pastor Rick Warren: Fighting Obesity with Faith," *Wall Street Journal*, January 14, 2014, https://tinyurl.com/y72t6nhj.

2. Wolfe, "Pastor Rick Warren."

3

THINNESS IS NOT NEXT TO GODLINESS

The night before my first day of college, I sobbed, head lying in my mom's lap as she brushed my hair back and reassured me. There were a variety of reasons I was crying; most were typical for a shy young woman headed off into something new. But I was also crying because I would be showing up at college still fat. My goal was to get a teaching degree and teach high school. By eighteen, I wasn't sure how I was going to lose weight. If I expected to spend my days standing in front of teenagers, I'd sure better look like someone who had her life together. In my mind (and in the narrative of much of our culture), a fat person definitely does not have her life together—her body a sign that surely something is very off.

It is not a spiritual strength to punish our body, but it took me years to learn that truth. As I tried and tried to become thin when I was younger, one of my mantras was "God is greater than my hunger." I believed that if I cared less for my body's natural physical reactions and more for God, then I would achieve a thin, godly body. I called hunger sinful desire, and feasting gluttony. Fatness was a sign of both.

My freshman year of college, I leaped into dieting with renewed vigor. I disciplined myself to count grapes and almonds and to measure food into predetermined serving sizes. A longtime friend I saw almost every day was also newly committed to dieting and exercise, so I had a partner for the struggle. Between my freshman year and my junior year of college, I did indeed lose some weight, partially due to the amount of walking I did around campus. I did not get thin, but I got smaller. I started dating my first boyfriend during my junior year of college, which reinforced the idea that being thinner would indeed bring other desired things into my life. That same year, however, I discovered fat acceptance, and I stopped counting my grapes.

I walked across the stage at my college graduation

in a graduation robe that I'd ordered in an appropriate size, with none of the anxiety I'd felt about my baptismal robe so many years before. A few months later, I interviewed for a teaching job and was handed the keys to room 214 in a high school about forty-five minutes from where I grew up. I decorated my room with excitement—adding bright pops of color about the room with literary posters and polka-dot bulletin board borders. On the first day of class, I wore a green dress with a hot-pink sweater. I was anything but invisible as I pushed the nerves down and told myself I could stand in front of these students and teach them about participial phrases, how to write a persuasive essay, and that we read literature so we can learn things from experiences we would not otherwise understand. There was nothing about my body's appearance that prevented me from teaching these academic principles, nothing about my rounded curves that meant I lacked the ability to communicate and educate. I had not managed to discipline myself into our culture's ideal body, but I had exhibited the self-discipline, wisdom, and intelligence needed to earn a college degree and a teaching certificate. That mattered more. Self-discipline and sacrifice show up in more ways than one. For someone who'd spent most of her life believing that the biggest indicator of whether or not I could be a mature and responsible adult was whether I managed to trim my waistline, this was revolutionary.

That first day, I sighed with satisfaction at the sight of my very own classroom and the fact that the thing I'd dreaded four years before—showing up in this space still fat—turned out to not be as scary as I had imagined it would be.

That year, I had an over-full room of freshman literature and composition students, many of whom had failed the course once or twice or three times before. Halfway through the fall semester, the students turned in their first major project. It was a disaster. They almost all failed. After speaking with my department chair, I came up with a plan to talk with them about how to effectively redo the assignment so they could learn the intended material. I opened the class by asking the students to write questions or make comments on the board while I took attendance at my desk and entered a few grades into the computer. In other words, the responses would be semi-anonymous to me, as I wouldn't be watching who was writing what on the board. This plan worked beautifully for my first three classes of the day. The students offered helpful feedback, owned their mistakes and where they had failed to follow directions, and clearly stated things I could do better to help them succeed.

By the time fourth period rolled around, I was feeling fairly confident in my ability to modify and creatively meet the needs of my students. I started the class as I had done three times before. When I finished taking attendance and looked at the board to begin another discussion on how we could all move forward together, I fell silent. Written in large letters across half the board was, "MAYBE IF YOU LOST WEIGHT YOU COULD TEACH BETTER." The snickers and giggles fell silent as I read the board with my back to the room. I could feel my face flame red and my pulse speed up. A couple of years into fat acceptance, I had grown in self-confidence, but this was still straight out of my nightmares. I paused, inhaled and exhaled a couple of slow, deep breaths, felt some of the red leave my face, and willed my voice to be calm and my mind to be clear as I turned to face my students. I gave a short speech that told them I had expected to have a productive conversation, as I'd had many times that day, but I was disappointed in their inability to be respectful. I assigned silent reading, told them I would be open to having the discussion as soon as someone demonstrated it was possible, and went back to my desk to continue grading papers.

I did not address the comment on the board specifically, something a younger version of myself would have felt the need to defend or acknowledge. I knew that I did not need to make my body look a certain way in order to deserve respect. I knew that self-discipline is displayed more in how we respond to disrespect and mistreatment from others than in how wide our hips spread. I do not need to force my body into a certain shape in order to deserve a position of authority, in order to demand that those around me treat me with respect.

After twenty long, silent minutes, one of my students stood up from her desk, walked to the board, and erased the comment. I thanked her for taking initiative, and we started again. This time, the conversation continued as it had most of the day—a productive way to address what the students needed to learn.

MAKING BODIES HOLY

For centuries, an idea has existed among some people of Christian faith that in order to become holy and good, the body must be conquered into submission. The body becomes less—both figuratively and literally—so that the soul can be free, purified, and holy. These beliefs are known as Gnosticism and asceticism. *Gnosticism* refers to "a variety of religious movements that stressed salvation through *gnosis*, or 'knowledge.'"[1] By the twentieth century, most scholars recognized Gnosticism as a heresy or even as a completely different religion from Christianity.[2]

One winter day, I spent a few hours exploring the ruins near Qumran in the south of Israel—the place where the Dead Sea Scrolls were found and an ancient home to an Essenes and gnostic community around the first century BCE. Throughout the ruins were several ritual baths, most with seven steps into them, as that is the holy number needed for part of the cleansing ritual. In the ruins, our tour guide pointed out the evidence of the way the community designed the architecture of the building in the midst of a desert to allow for access to running water—needed for the frequent ritual cleansing. Bodily purity was of high importance, and great efforts were made to ensure that the community would have not just what they needed for survival but also what they believed they needed for their bodies to be pure and holy.

Gnosticism denies the importance of the body God created. We know God values the body—it is created in God's image, Jesus showed up on earth in a body, and over and over throughout Scripture, bodies are valued and cared for. Our bodies take a

central role in how we live our lives. Gnosticism suggests that bodies are evil and must be conquered.
"Gnosticism developed [the idea] that a heavenly
spirit, acting independently of the good God,
formed the material world and trapped human spirits in material bodies. The moral life must therefore
be one of asceticism, denying the body and its
desires."[3]

Fundamental to the understanding of Gnosticism
is the idea of dualism. At its root, dualism is not a
religious doctrine; it simply references the notion of
two opposing ideas. In this case, however, dualism
refers to the belief that our physical bodies represent
the material/evil world and our soul represents the
spiritual/good world. This sets up a battle between
the two, where the soul is supposed to conquer and
subdue the body.

This belief says that our bodies are evil, they must
be conquered, and that since the body and the
mind/soul are separate things, they can be treated
independently of each other. This belief elevates the
suffering of our bodies as a means of becoming holy.
This theology can advocate for suffering at our
own hands through self-deprivation and harm.
Christians who view extreme dieting and exercise
regimens (that prioritize thinness) as good spiritual
discipline are often espousing this kind of dualist

gnostic thinking. Gnostic dualism is the same faulty foundational idea that allows for the belief that abuse or slavery could be a way to strengthen one's faith.

Mayra Rivera, professor of religion and Latina/o studies at Harvard Divinity School, argues that we are getting better and better at finding ways to transform our bodies into what is considered socially acceptable. Products and procedures that change our hair, our skin color, and the functionality of our gastrointestinal organs are all marketed as ways we can be a better version of ourselves. Rivera summarizes: "The images of bodies thus produced are never simply external to ourselves; their very power depends on their capacity to shape our desires and compel us to see ourselves through and conform to them—to incarnate the ideal body."[4] I often hear people say they are changing their bodies for themselves. They want to feel better about themselves and like what they see in the mirror. I believe that they are honest in their self-perception, that they believe they are focusing only on their personal preferences, but I believe that much more is at work there. We live in a culture that tells us so much about what a desirable body looks like that we are compelled to see our bodies through that false ideal.

The response of Christians afraid their body

makes them look like they lead undisciplined lives has long been to engage in food deprivation or to otherwise cause intentional pain for the body: *asceticism*. Ascetics withdraw from all worldly pleasures in an effort to purify the soul. Historically, it is a response to the fear of being, or being perceived as, a glutton. (I'll explore more of what gluttony is and is not in the next chapter.) Our Christian cultural obsession with disciplining our bodies in an attempt to look holy means that bodies that do not conform to this discipline are read as unholy by contrast. Thin-preference may not have begun within the Christian church, but the church has done little or nothing to combat it. Just as race, ethnicity, and gender have been used to define moral and spiritual superiority and inferiority throughout history, body size and one's attempts to conform to the ideal or not also carry connotations of inferiority or superiority.

The Desert Fathers and Mothers were a group of Christian monks and others who lived in the Egyptian desert. Their life and teachings became the foundation of much of the monastic tradition. One of them in the fourth century, Evagrius of Pontus, participated in an ascetic regimen and said gluttony is the "nourishment of evil thoughts, laziness in fasting, . . . receptacle of disease, . . . pollution of the intellect, weakness of the body, . . . gloomy death."[5]

Asceticism, a manifestation of gnostic thought, seeks to cure gluttony by subduing the body through deprivation or pain in order to make the soul pure and free from the presumed sinful constraints and desires of the body.

While we don't often call it asceticism anymore, modern diet culture is not much different. Our diets are all about becoming slimmer and less. Every January, we are bombarded with messaging proclaiming that for a new year, we need a new us—a thinner us. Gym advertisements try to convince us that without pain, there is no gain, and that our sweat is our fat crying out. We tell ourselves that we will pay for a sweet indulgence later with a workout that will leave us breathless and wobbly legged. There is nothing wrong with exerting our bodies to their limits; that is one way of living an active, vibrant, embodied life. But when we push our bodies to painful limits because we believe our sinful, wayward bodies deserve pain and punishment, we are participating in that ancient tradition of gnostic asceticism that seeks to separate the body from the soul.

As much as it is possible, exercise and movement should be about enjoying our body or at least its productive efforts. While there have been years of my life when I sat out from physical activities, convinced I would hamper others' ability to enjoy themselves, I learned the joy of movement in deep and meaningful ways during the years I lived as a houseparent. I entered into that time committed to modeling healthy body image for the eight teenage girls under my care. On one of our first nights together, we walked the few blocks to Lake Michigan from our home in a Chicago suburb and played simple childhood games like red rover on the sand. Once, we were unloading supplies from our car, and I sashayed up the sidewalk, balancing a new boxed vacuum on my head, held in place with one arm raised high while I carried something smaller in the other hand. The girls were amused (and I think a little impressed) at my strength. When the snows came, my southern self discovered I really *loved* shoveling snow. This began my love of what I call purposeful movement. I put in an hour of aerobic exercise scraping the heavy, wet snow off the sidewalks around our house, and at the end of it, I got passable sidewalks and a driveway we could easily pull into and out of. I was similarly enthralled with the walkability of Chicago. I have no need for a treadmill when I can actually go somewhere with my feet.

Not every physical activity I threw myself into worked out well. On one of my last nights with this community, after almost three years together, we went to a place that was full of trampolines. We jumped and bounced to our heart's content with peals of laughter. The girls were enjoying the foam pit—a deep pit filled with large blocks of foam that you could jump into from whatever height you could manage to achieve from the nearby trampoline. I eyed the pit with caution, carefully watching the exit strategy of those before me. I decided to go for it and launched myself into the pit. I immediately realized I was stuck. Others had piled the foam blocks beneath their feet to create a stairway out of the pit, pulling themselves up and out over the edge. I had miscalculated just how much the foam would compress under my weight. No matter how many foam blocks I corralled around and under me, I could not get enough height to get out, and I lacked the upper-body strength needed to pull myself out. I willed myself to stay calm and not spiral into a panic attack. It did, truly, feel for a few terrifying seconds as if I would never get out. Truthfully, I was just embarrassed. Two of the girls I worked with jumped in and helped push me out. I calmed down my breathing as I welcomed the news that I was not going to spend the rest of my life in the pit of foam, and then I went back to jumping with joy on the much more accessible trampolines. I was thankful that it was not the first time I had intentionally sought to be active in front of the girls, thankful even that they saw me deal with a situation that proved too much for the size of my body and then continue on. My body does not deserve punishment because it weighs enough to compress foam; my body needed some help from my community, a couple of minutes to recover, and then some joyful jumping once again.

Susan Bordo, author of *The Unbearable Weight: Feminism, Western Culture, and the Body*,[6] talks about eating disorders and how both the size and shape of female bodies is intrinsically linked to what we think about goodness and womanhood in our culture. She focuses on the idea that we often desire hard, definite lines on our bodies. We want angular jaws, flat stomachs that show the outlines of well-defined muscles, toned calves, and biceps. The soft, rounded corners of a double chin or the way fat causes the skin to rise and fall in a gentle slope has no place. Those noncommittal curves with no hard lines or points are undefined and undesired.

Bordo points out that people who struggle with eating disorders exhibit gnostic dualistic thinking about their body: "The body is the enemy . . . [and] all that threatens our attempts at control."[7] As a result, the body becomes the source and site of battles where one must conquer the body in order to free the soul. Anorexia is an extreme but all-too-common disease in which someone disciplines or punishes their body through exercise and food restriction in order to make their body smaller and smaller. In extreme cases, anorexia causes the body to waste away, becoming the smallest it can possibly be, sometimes even to death. To have this diminished body is thus the ultimate separation of soul from body. In this disordered way of thinking, there is literally too much body present on a person. While people may reassure average-size or thin anorexics that their body does not need to be reduced, fat people are often told there their body is indeed too much.

While anorexia is an extreme and complicated disease, the idea that thinness is evidence of a disciplined and controlled body prevails throughout our culture. We watch television shows (such as *The Biggest Loser*) in which large bodies are subjected to intense regimes of discipline and restriction in order to achieve a more desirable size. (A body that likely won't stay that size, due in part to the fact that the weight-loss method promoted on the show causes weight gain to a higher weight than when the person started.[8]) We declare a war on obesity with the goal of eradicating a certain body from the face of the planet. On any given day, one can read the news online and find a headline that exalts the many-pound weight loss of some ordinary person or celebrity. A thin body is praised as disciplined and triumphant. A fat body is deemed to be too much for this world and should be eliminated.

There is nothing on my body that is flat and straight. There never has been. I have been fat since childhood. There have been many days where I have stood staring at the reflection of my naked body in a tall mirror, stretching and holding the heavy drapes of skin and muscle and fat that hang from my stomach, chin, and arms. I wonder what it looks and feels like for someone whose body does not drape and roll. I do not know what a body of angles feels like; all of my corners have been well padded for as long as I can remember.

I used to hate these parts of my body, looking at them in the mirror only long enough to grab the offending curves in disgust in an attempt to smooth them flat and get an idea for what my goal should be. I'd spread my hands across my jawbone and down to my chin, smoothing back the skin until it was tight and pulled at the corners of my lips and eyes, and stare at this thinner, taut version of myself. The image reflected back to me was an idea of what I could look like when I made my body into what it was supposed to be. These days, I am thankful that when I take the time to stop and look in the mirror, my eyes and mind are gentler.

As I began to change my thinking, after discovering fat acceptance, I worked to accept my body. "This is my body," I whispered to myself as I stared at my reflection. "My body looks like this, and it still moves and laughs and lives and loves." After a few years, when I was used to seeing my body, when I recognized her folds and rolls and dimples, I began working to love my body. I lathered lotion up and down my arms and legs, across my stomach and chest, discovering the way my skin felt, where it was warm or heavy or soft. I marveled at the muscles in my calves that were impressive but invisible to anyone else under their cushion of fat. It took a while longer, but eventually I did not just accept my body but loved it. Loved my curves and my warmth and my strength. Loved all of my expansiveness that took up space in a world that frequently demands I disappear.

Undoing Gnosticism

When I first started exploring the idea of fat acceptance, I had to detox my relationship with my body, eliminating its ingrained ascetic beliefs. For a few months, I did not follow any rule but instant gratification. I ate what I wanted and did the physical activity I wanted, or not. I don't recommend this method, but it is a common story that I hear from others who have made the transition.

This did not last very long, for a few reasons. First, a hedonistic life was not my goal. I knew I wanted a holistically healthy relationship with both food and my body, and this period of no rules was just the way I needed to reset my brain. In addition, part of fat acceptance, and more specifically, the Health at Every Size framework,[9] is learning to eat and move and live intuitively. After a few weeks of not paying attention to anything, I started to be intentional about noting my energy levels and mood after eating a particular thing or after a day of activity or rest. I thought about the food I ate and whether I had enjoyed it or not—its taste, texture, temperature. I learned things about myself: I really, really like vegetables. I have very little interest in any chocolate that isn't super dark. Arugula, beets, and goat cheese may be the world's most perfect flavor combination, followed closely by super-dark chocolate and sea salt. I love purposeful movement—that is, physical activity that accomplishes something beyond exercise. I noted that if I ate fast food, I was sluggish a few hours later or even the next day. When I had a salad with lots of veggies and a protein and a vinaigrette, I thoroughly enjoyed the process of preparing it and felt better later. Sometimes I still eat fast food because sometimes convenience wins or it is something I am craving. However, on days when I need comfort food that will make my body exhale in the pure joy and fulfillment of it all, I chop veggies and mix up a dressing with whatever vinegar and citrus I have lying around.

This practice of eating intuitively and choosing food that is satisfying in the moment—and to which the body responds well—is the antidote to asceticism. I am not punishing my body; I am honoring it. I am more holistically healthy because of this. Despite the brief period of detox, when I indulged to excess, I quickly learned that I did not need to eat dessert just because it was available. When the focus on food had been that some food was bad and some was good, eating bad food seemed like I was getting away with something, so I did not want to pass up the opportunity. When I operated out of that mentality, a scarcity mentality, I had cake whenever it was offered and available. In a relationship with food based on intuition about what my body needs and the knowledge that cake is not morally bad because of its calorie count, I can choose to eat cake or not for other reasons. I can pass if I am not hungry, not in the mood for cake, if it's not a flavor I enjoy, or any other number of reasons. There will be cake another day. I did not miss my chance. I do not need an excuse to eat cake.

Many years into learning to eat intuitively and having a holistic relationship with my fat body, I shared an apartment with three other women in Philadelphia. One spring, as Lent approached, my housemate Emily knocked on my door and asked, "I heard Lent was coming up. Have anything you want to give up? Get rid of? Get out of your cabinets? Sweets? Would you like to give me your sweets?" I laughed and told her that I wasn't giving them up, but I didn't have many in my cabinet anyway. Another housemate, Susan, called from around the corner, "You know Nicole doesn't have sweets! Ask her for some vegetables! She's got plenty of those."

When Susan laughed off Emily's request as if it was absurd that I would have a cabinet full of sweets to unload, I knew I had achieved a goal. My friends and housemates—the people who did life with me—saw part of the authentic me, not who the world says I am based on my body size. I am not a better person because I like vegetables, but that is a much more descriptive and accurate understanding of me than the standard media portrayal of a fat person who eats and desires only sweets and potato chips. For Susan to know that about me was a moment when I realized I was living a more authentic life. For many years, I had eaten junk food because I thought that was expected of me. I didn't know what I actually liked; I didn't know what food gave me delight and energy. Turns out, it's more likely to be arugula than ice cream—though ice cream is still pretty awesome, too!

To avoid falling into gnostic dualism or a tendency to asceticism, we must first honor our bodies as critical parts of who we are and how we live our lives and faith. This starts with understanding that our bodies are made and loved by God, just as they are. We were not created as spirits first and then encumbered with our bodies after sin entered into the picture. Rather, our bodies were created and filled with the breath, the spirit, of God. When sin came, so did shame and fear about bodies.

It is true that there are food-related ways to sin with our bodies, so we must learn to differentiate between gluttony, feasting, and fatness (more on that in the next chapter). Dualism makes our faith too simple and easy. All we have to worry about is conquering our individual body into submission. But holy lives require much more. God created our bodies and called the people of God to community. Communal faith means we have to know what is happening to our neighbors. We have to know if our choices hurt someone else, and then we have do the work of repentance to bring our thoughts and actions into alignment with a God who wants us all invited to the feasting table. That is a much higher standard for pure faith than simply being able to declare ourselves disciplined, godly, and thin.

Notes

1. Edwin M. Yamauchi, "Gnosticism," in *Dictionary of New Testament Background*, ed. Craig A. Evans and Stanley E. Porter (Downers Grove, IL: InterVarsity, 2000), 414.

2. Yamauchi, "Gnosticism," 416.

3. David J. Atkinson and David H. Field, eds., *New Dictionary of Christian Ethics and Pastoral Theology* (Downers Grove, IL: InterVarsity, 1995), 323.

4. Mayra Rivera, "Unsettling Bodies," *Journal of Feminist Studies in Religion* 26, no. 2 (September 2010): 120.

5. Teresa M. Shaw, *The Burden of the Flesh: Feasting and Sexuality in Early Christianity* (Minneapolis: Fortress Press, 1998), cited in Francine Prose, *Gluttony: The Seven Deadly Sins* (Oxford: Oxford University Press, 2003).

6. Susan Bordo, *Unbearable Weight: Feminism, Western*

Culture, and the Body (Berkeley: University of California Press, 1993).

7. Bordo, *Unbearable Weight*, 145.

8. Erin Fothergill et al., "Persistent Metabolic Adaptation 6 Years after 'The Biggest Loser' Competition," *Obesity* 24, no. 8 (2016): 1612–19.

9. Health at Every Size and HAES are registered trademarks of the Association for Size Diversity and Health (ASDAH). More information is available at www.sizediversityandhealth.org.

4

COMPARING
FATNESS AND
GLUTTONY

When I was twenty-seven, I scheduled my first appointment with a therapist. I booked the appointment one morning after a sleepless night because I couldn't stop worrying. That night, I couldn't shake the feeling that I had forgotten to do something important or had done something wrong and it would mess things up. I hadn't made a mistake or forgotten anything, but my anxiety would not let me rest. When I sat down in the chair in the therapist's office, the wooden arms pushed painfully into the sides of my hips, but I was too nervous to move to the nearby couch. Plus, the firmness and structure of the chair felt safer than the plushness of the overstuffed couch as I gathered the courage to share deep fears. My therapist asked, "Why are you here?" I told her about my anxiety and sleepless nights and things from the past that still weighed heavy on my mind. At the end of our hour, she looked at me and asked, "How long have you struggled with your weight?"

I took a moment to gather my thoughts and replied, "I don't. I believe in Health at Every Size. I do my best to eat healthy and stay active and accept my body as it is." To her credit, my therapist never mentioned it again, after explaining that she wanted to ask because food addiction is a common side effect of many mental illnesses. On the rest of my visits over the next two years, I chose the softer, wider, and less painful couch over the armchair. She and I worked through some of the root causes of my anxiety, and I am thankful both that I said something to her and that she listened and worked with me on my actual issues.

My therapist assumed that I was addicted to food—that I was gluttonous—based on the size of my body. Certainly, I have had moments of gluttony related to food. Sometimes I eat my feelings in unhealthy ways. Yet, I do think it is also possible to eat emotionally in healthy ways. Sometimes food is a way to embrace feelings of joy (birthday cake!)

or sadness (your favorite, comforting soup). I agree, though, that using food as an escape from reality on a regular basis can be unhealthy. But that does not always mean that someone will become fat, and using food as regular means of escape from problems has never been my problem. My weight is a combination of many things, including genetics, a low-income childhood where we ate a lot of cheap processed food, and a personality that is more than content to read or sew or hide away in my home for an entire weekend. That is to say, my fatness is not a sign of gluttony.

Being accused of gluttony puts me in good company. Jesus, from his early days, was known to associate with those who were deemed to be full of shame because of cultural norms and ideals. Jesus was called a glutton (Luke 7), so our ability to identify this sin in others is not as cut-and-dried as we'd like to think. Turns out, you can't see it in someone else, even if they are feasting to excess and hanging out with other people who act the same.

While the conventional understanding of gluttony is simply overeating, from what I see in Scripture, gluttony is in fact consumption at the expense of someone else, especially the poor and marginalized. Christianity is about loving God and our neighbors. There is no room in that commandment for an obsessive regard for the size of our body, but there is plenty of room to pay attention to how our actions affect others. That includes being able to identify ways in which consumption breaks community and harms others, so that we know when we are overconsuming at the expense of others. This requires a communal faith rather than an individual faith.

Food is a necessary part of our life, and it can beautifully connect us both to our neighbors and to God. Yet from early on, this God-given gift of hunger and food plays a role in the way the people of God fail to love themselves or each other well, falling instead into gluttony. Gluttony is not feasting. Gluttony is not fatness. We can just as easily be a thin glutton as we can be a fat person who is not prone to gluttony. Gluttony is the consumption of food at the expense of others. If racism is prejudice plus power, gluttony is overconsumption plus power.

FATNESS IN THE OLD TESTAMENT

A few times in the Old Testament, the Scriptures equate being overfed with being fat and being oppressive. In these cases, fatness is used in the Scriptures as a metaphor or satire or both. While it is true that using fatness in this way is a literary tool I do not appreciate, the Bible is certainly full of cultural metaphors and commonalities that we resist using today for various sound social and theological reasons. To use biblical instances of fatness as a proof text on why fatness is bad is inaccurate and misses the actual sin pointed out in the passages. In the context of the ancient world, fatness was highly correlated to privilege and power. Such simple correlations no longer exist in the contemporary Western world. Though there still remain problematic disparities between abundance and famine, fatness in the Western world does not solely reside on the hips of the powerful. In fact, in the Western world, it is those with the least amount of privilege and power who are most likely to be fat.

In Judges 3, we learn the story of King Eglon of Moab, who is "a very fat man" and has ruled over the Israelites for eighteen years.[1] The Israelites, not a fan of Eglon's oppressive rule, cry out to God for deliverance. Because those under Eglon's oppressive rule face hunger, his fatness is damning. The climax of the story is when a man named Ehud takes a sword, finds Eglon alone in the bathroom, and then thrusts his dagger into Eglon. The fat of the king's belly swallows the sword, handle and all, before bursting open and spilling his intestines onto the ground. Eglon dies. The detail of Eglon's fat swallowing the sword fits well in the gruesome humor of the story (literally bathroom humor).

Before we hear the story of Eglon's death, we learn the way he lived and ruled. Eglon lived in the cool chambers of his palace with plenty to eat, while his subjects lived in hunger on the barren hills of the countryside. Eglon's fatness is mentioned when he is judged, yes. But he is not being judged for his fatness; he is being judged for his oppression. Eglon was not killed because he was fat. Nor was he evil and oppressive because he was fat. Eglon's sin was corruption and oppression.

Notice for a moment that a really fat man exists in the Bible, and there is nothing in the text to indicate that this was the only fat person that people had ever seen. Fatness existed in the ancient Near East. Fatness is not a modern invention. Fatness is not the end of the world.

The story of Eglon is not the only place where gluttony shows up in the Bible. Growing up in church, I frequently heard the story of Sodom and Gomorrah. Abraham bargained with God to save the city if Abraham could find just a small number of righteous people, even ten. God approved, yet the city and almost all of its inhabitants were destroyed. I was taught that the sin of Sodom was homosexuality. Yet we learn in Ezekiel that the sin of Sodom was that they were overfed and unconcerned for the poor (Ezekiel 16:49). The Message translation says it this way: "The sin of your sister Sodom was this: She lived with her daughters in the lap of luxury—proud, gluttonous, and lazy. They ignored the oppressed and the poor. They put on airs and lived obscene lives." If we look back at the story of Sodom in Genesis 19, we see the sexual immorality. The people of the town demand that the guests in Lot's house come out, because they view the guests as sexual commodities to be used as they wish. Lot is no better, offering up his daughters instead. This is oppressive behavior. Yes, sexual sin is part of the oppressive behavior, but it is a result of being "proud, gluttonous, and lazy." That gluttony looks like oppression of visitors and women, not like fatness. In verse 13, the reason the guests at Lot's house give for the fact that the town is about to be destroyed is that "the outcry to the Lord against its people is so great that he has sent us to destroy it" (NIV). The Message says, "The outcries of victims here to God are deafening." God has heard the cry of the oppressed—those under Eglon's rule and those who suffered in Sodom—and sides with them against those who consume resources or other people's bodies for their own benefit. Sodom broke community with its gluttony, as did Eglon. They oppressed others.

In Deuteronomy, we read:

> Jeshurun grew fat and kicked;
>   filled with food, they became heavy and
>   sleek.
> They abandoned the God who made them
>   and rejected the Rock their Savior. . . .
> The Lord saw this and rejected them
>   because he was angered by his sons and
>   daughters.
> (Deuteronomy 32:15, 19, NIV)

This passage is from a song describing Israel's backsliding. "Jeshurun" is not a person but Israel as a whole. It is not likely that every single person in Israel had grown fat. Instead, this use of fatness is again metaphorical.

Deuteronomy 32:15 begins the second stanza of a song and focuses on how Israel has abandoned God. In the presence of abundant food, the Israelites overconsume and take the generosity of God for granted. The fatness of Israel is not an indictment against fatness but an indictment against overconsumption and pursuit of material blessing, rather than pursuing God. Instead of praising the God who is generous and provides many great things, they gorge themselves on the benevolence and then get mad at the provider. Renowned biblical scholar Walter Brueggemann says, "Israel's condition was one of satiation: fat, bloated, gorged. Israel was no longer needy and could not remember its dependence upon YHWH. This sorry condition expressed itself as the violation of the first commandment. Israel embraced other loyalties and other ways of securing its own existence."[2] Their lack of trust in God's provision, not their fatness, is the reason for God's lament over Israel. Again, as with Eglon, my modern sensibilities mean I wish the Scripture used a different metaphor. But the truth that is being taught is not a judgment against fatness; it is a judgment against the Israelites' sin and their lack of trust.

The author of Proverbs 23 advises those seeking wisdom to avoid the consumption of the king's food: "Do not desire his delicacies, for they are deceptive food" (Proverbs 23:3, ESV). The proverb does not go into much detail about why the king's food is deceptive, but the broader context of Scripture (and our knowledge of the world in general) shows us that rulers can use food as a way to oppress others. Kings feast while the people starve. Those of us with financial resources and social influence consume our preferred food, despite its cost to the environment or those who grow it. This is not about fatness; this is about justice.

In Psalm 73, we see a description of arrogant men. The psalmist writes:

> I was envious of the arrogant
> when I saw the prosperity of the wicked.
> For they have no pangs until death;
> their bodies are fat and sleek.
> They are not in trouble as others are;
> they are not stricken like the rest of
> [human]kind.
>
> (Psalm 73:3–5, ESV)

Again, those described as arrogant and prosperous are described as having fat bodies. Here, the fat bodies are a descriptor of a body that has no pain or suffering. They are well nourished and healthy, but they have gotten that way by taking advantage of their neighbors. They are guilty of gluttony because their prosperity comes from wickedness, not because they are fat. Scripture describes them as people who "have no struggles; their bodies are healthy and strong" (Psalm 73:4, NIV). Near the end of Psalm 73, the psalmist proclaims, "My flesh and my heart may fail, / but God is the strength of my heart and my portion forever" (73:26, ESV). I imagine that he is calling out to God for strength in the midst of literal hunger. The wicked have taken the food meant for all and hoarded it for themselves. It is detrimental to the health of those around them.

Food is a necessary part of our day, and the temptation to misuse it is strong. The Scripture record does not unilaterally show that gluttonous consumption is tied to fat people, so we should not assume that fatness comes from gluttony or that you will become fat if given to gluttony. Not all wicked people in the Bible are described as fat. At times, the writers of the Scriptures used the metaphor, and other times, they describe the wicked as seemingly invincible. No body type reveals our character or our faith—not in the Bible, and not today.

It is good to question whether our food choices hurt others. It is good to question whether our food restrictions are contributing to a culture of shame. It is good to question whether we are consuming food in an effort to satisfy a need that only God can fill. It is good to question whether our comments around the dinner table or before the slicing of the birthday cake are contributing to someone else's shame.

There are many ways to please God in our consumption: be mindful that God is our provider, honor the moments for feasting, and love our neighbors by not consuming in a way that oppresses them.

Enjoy the church potluck, and be intentional to not comment on its perceived impact on your waistline (or someone else's!). At communal meals, allow others the freedom to fill their plates without commenting or judging. This includes seconds. Do not assume that others want to lose twenty pounds and would love to hear about the latest diet promising an easy path to that goal. We as a church and as individual Christians still often struggle to live into the call to love God and neighbors and enemies too, but a focus on that calling is a much better place to start our journey to living faithful lives than to turn our eyes inward and judge our faith by how disciplined our body appears.

GLUTTONY IN THE EARLY CHURCH

It should come as no surprise to anyone that our understandings of and opinions about bodies have changed drastically in the approximately two thousand years since Jesus walked this earth. Gluttony is considered one of the seven deadly sins, a concept that is less familiar to Protestants than to Catholic or Orthodox believers. The notion of these seven deadly, or capital, sins does not have its origin in the Bible. Lists of capital sins most likely began in the fourth century with the Desert Fathers. The sins are pride, envy, anger, sloth, greed, gluttony, and lust; they are thought to be base sins—that is, the broad categories, which can be detailed and specified to cover quite the range of sins. Gluttony, along with lust, is considered a carnal sin, a perversion of the physical desires.

Gluttony has an impact on community. Selfish consumption demands food as soon as hunger strikes (or before) rather than waiting for a shared mealtime, requires costly or highly complicated dishes, or takes more than enough from the plate that is passed to serve others. These gluttonous, self-absorbed behaviors do not include the very real and legitimate dietary needs that people may need to manage because of disease or other circumstances. In such cases, the gluttonous response is insisting on a meal that fails to accommodate the needs of those present. Avoiding gluttony requires paying attention to your neighbors. It's a lot harder than just checking the scale each morning.

I was once a part of a church small group that included a woman with Crohn's disease, long before gluten-free was household language. I offered to cook dinner for the group one night. I delight in making sure that the table is a place everyone can gather. Whenever possible, I make one meal that everyone can enjoy. So I spent a couple of weeks scouring the internet for recipes that were both gluten free and delicious. In the grocery-store aisle, I examined the ingredients in mustard, checking to see if I could use that particular brand. On the night we had dinner, we all shared a common meal. This attention to detail, which welcomes and includes rather than excludes, is not gluttony.

There will, of course, be times when food restrictions compete with each other, so that a common meal is not possible. Eating the same dish is never a requirement; potlucks are beautiful things. But the idea is to do what is most welcoming, what is most inclusive. Gluttony can be difficult to avoid. It requires paying attention to our neighbors and knowing those with whom we share community. When our desire for a quick and easy meal trumps our neighbors' medical needs, we are being gluttonous. When our desire to follow all the in-fashion rules of how we might achieve bodily purity comes before considering the resources available or accessible to others, that is gluttonous. Gluttony prevents or inhibits our ability to dine together as believers in Christ. It prevents our ability to share from a common table where the bread is broken and passed around.

Our obsession with weight as an indicator of gluttony is mostly a contemporary one. While fatness has indicated wealth and stature in many civilizations throughout history, the resulting implications about the person who is fat have changed. Gluttony, like everything else, is contextual. When civilization entered the Industrial Age, the economic divide separated those with resources from those who had less. Those who could afford to eat were thought of as successful. Indulging in food to the extent that it shows up on one's body was a mark of pride, not shame. In this same era, there was also a rise in a concern with health, longevity, and medicine. People began to question the food we eat and our weights. Diets—a privilege of those who had more than enough—became popular.

If gluttony is overconsumption at the expense of others, then the opposite of gluttony is mindful consumption. This is what we are called to. It can seem impossible to consume in our globalized world without oppressing someone. However, that does not mean we cannot make the effort and do better when we know better. We are called to feast as part of a community of believers that welcomes everyone. We are called to care about the way the food makes it to our table, because the food production system involves the lives and realities of other people created in the image of God. (And, for that matter, so is the way the table makes its way to our house.

Oppression of workers is not limited to the food industry.)

A number of years ago, I discovered quinoa, but then I backed away from using it often, once I learned that its popularity in the United States is causing economic devastation for the farmers who have been producing the crop to feed their communities for centuries. I have learned about the horrors of factory-farmed animals and the way both non-human creatures and humans are treated in violent, undignified ways in order to get a cheap hamburger or an inexpensive Thanksgiving turkey to my plate. I have heard the calls from those who pick strawberries and tomatoes, asking us to not buy them for a bit while they ask the farm owners for fairer compensation and work conditions, so for a time, I only ate strawberries I picked from the farm down the road and bypassed the fast-food restaurant that had refused to sign the fair-labor pledge for the tomato pickers. I scan the grocery store and find the cheap bundle of kale instead of the one in the trendy package, because I have learned about the gentrifying prices of food—the way a food that has been a staple of low-income families for decades suddenly becomes too expensive to buy because it got trendy. If I can help keep the cheap kale in stock by increasing the customer demand and leaving the other on the shelf, I hope I am doing my part to resist this injustice. In all of these, I take the time to question how my demand for food, especially out-of-season or trendy food, has an impact on my global neighbors.

It is hard. There are overlapping intersections that crisscross on top of each other. I can get lost trying to decide if quinoa or chicken is the least oppressive choice. Food from the once-a-week farmers' market may be the best option, but it is not always the one I choose, for a variety of reasons, convenience among them. I am not always consistent. I don't always make the choices I want to make, but I do try to be mindful of the ways the choices on my plate affect my global neighbors and all of creation. This is how we avoid gluttony. This is how we honor our call to love God and neighbors. I recommend picking one way you can make more mindful choices about where your food comes from and starting there. Attempting to completely change overnight the way you get your food will most likely set you up for failure.

I think God wants us to care more about whether the food on our plate steals from or hurts a neighbor than whether it makes our thighs touch. Making choices that push back against gluttony is much more complicated than not eating ice cream. This focus on others keeps us connected to community, reminding us that the world is wider than the size of our waistline.

NOTES

1. This section on King Eglon is based on a blog post I first published on my website: J. Nicole Morgan, "Fat King Eglon and Scapegoating Our Guilt," September 25, 2014, https://tinyurl.com/ya2kmgyw.

2. Walter Brueggemann, *Deuteronomy* (Nashville: Abingdon, 2001), 279.

5

HONORING THE TEMPLE

The summer after my junior year of high school, I spent a week in London on a mission trip with about a hundred other youth from churches across the United States. After a couple of days of sightseeing in London, we began the work we came to do, dividing into teams and spreading out across the city to serve and minister to the people of London. I was on a prayer team whose goal was to support the work of a local missionary by prayer-walking the streets of communities that were primarily home to immigrants. We stopped and talked with shop owners and people on the street. We told them a little bit about the church the missionary worked with and asked if we could pray for them about anything. Then we went on our way.

I walked the streets of London that week in a fat body. Aside from being a tad bit cramped in the tiny European shower stalls of our dorm-lodging, my body size did not affect my ability to talk and walk and pray at all. At that point in my life, however, I fully expected my body to hamper my ability to serve God. The messages I had heard and internalized about fat bodies and serving God taught me that my body would fail in this mission. I would fail either because I would be physically incapable of performing some task or because my fatness would reveal me to be someone who did not love God and would be unable to effectively serve others.

About eighteen months before my trip to London, my almost-sixteen-year-old self wrote in my journal, "I need to lose weight, not just for myself, but because my weight can hinder me from God's will. It's like any other sin that separates you from God. Let me explain. I know with all my heart that God wants me involved in missions and on mission teams. The problem I face with my sin is that I would not physically be able to complete some mission trips. If I had been able to go I would have given that extra word or that extra smile to someone and that would have given them the last push to Jesus, but because of my sinful gluttony they may never come to God. . . . If my sin gets in the way I cannot be used in his PERFECT will. I want so bad to be in good shape for personal reasons, but I finally realize that it is important for God's will too." This was followed immediately by a passionate description of my disbelief that my brother had gotten a tattoo. I had a lot of rules about bodies and which ones could serve God well and which ones couldn't.

I had internalized the messages I heard from church that taught I needed to honor my body so that I could live long and serve God. The often unspoken but sometimes explicit message was that if your body wasn't ideal, you weren't really honoring God, and you therefore couldn't be a messenger for God. The verses about honoring our bodies as temples become weapons against persons whose bodies who do not meet current cultural norms.

I frequently wrestled with the question of how I could actively serve God in a fat body. At the same time, I believed that God's grace is greater than my sin of fatness. This belief, and a bit of a stubborn streak, propelled me to sign up for the mission trip even though I wasn't sure how well I would fit on the plane.

Despite navigating the streets of London with physical ease and having no one refuse to listen to me on account of my fatness, I still assumed my fatness was a barrier to doing God's work in the world.

As I realized that I was, in fact, serving God, that my thunder thighs moved me along the sidewalks just fine, I prayed somber prayers of thanks—thanking God for the grace of using me despite the way my body screamed failure. I also knew that such a life could not be my future. I knew I could not make plans to travel to London or any other city beyond the bounds of the United States and be a full-time missionary. Not with the denomination of which I was a part, at least. Not officially. In the Southern Baptist Convention, there was a weight limit for international missionaries: a body mass index (BMI) limit based on a chart from their health insurance company. I'd have to lose a significant amount of weight to qualify. Despite years of trying, that didn't seem possible.

I don't remember first learning about this missionary weight limit, whether I read it in some pamphlet or heard it from a visiting missionary who was home on furlough to rest and raise support. It is, like most assumptions about thinness and a better life, just something that seems to have always been a part of my psyche—a ruler against which I measured my body and my worth.

On one of the last nights of the mission trip, the team met in the upstairs room of an old stone church in London whose wood floorboards creaked as we walked in. There was masking tape running in long lines on the floor, dividing the room into quadrants. We were told to sit anywhere.

After we sang, we had a time for prayer. The leader told us to look down and notice in which quadrant we were sitting. These four quadrants, he said, represented the four hemispheres of the globe. We were instructed to pray for the people who lived in that hemisphere. I was sitting in the North West: Canada, Mexico, and the United States. As I prayed that night, I felt—in that earnest way that teenagers feel important things—as if this were not just my calling for prayer that night, but my calling for life. The idea began to form in my head that I was called not to a place outside the borders of the United States, but rather to the people whom I call fellow citizens. My memories of childhood are filled with the stories of missionaries who served around the world and the belief that I would do something similar. That dream disappeared almost overnight after that night in London.

The next Fourth of July, I sat on the grass in my hometown, and as the fireworks blasted through the sky, I stared at my neighbors surrounding me. My stomach filled with butterflies as I felt the anxiety of the realization that these were my people—the ones to whom I felt called. My life has continued, in

unexpected ways, to maintain this call. I've taught
Bible studies out of almost every home in which I've
lived. I've served in schools and nonprofits, attended
seminary, and joined community groups. My most
passionate calling to the church in America is to
urge Christians to let go of body shame in the pursuit of living fully and vibrantly into who God has
called us to be.

Yet I still wonder if I turned what was just supposed to be a night of prayer into a lifelong calling
because I didn't think I had another option. Because
I wasn't sure if I would ever be able to achieve the
body I needed in order to do what I really wanted
at the time: go to a different country. I assumed my
denomination was right, that my fat body could not
handle the situations that living in other countries
might present.

The next time I boarded a flight that crossed an
ocean was almost sixteen years after my trip to London. I landed in Tel Aviv, Israel, and spent a week
mostly in the West Bank, visiting with Palestinian
Christians.

One day, we visited the Nassar family farm called
Tent of Nations, near Bethlehem. The land has
belonged to a Palestinian Christian family for generations, and they are fighting to hold on to it despite
settlements popping up all around. Settlements are

illegal homes and other buildings for Israelis built on land that is supposed to belong to Palestinians. The Israelis had bulldozed the olive trees on the farm just a couple of years prior and had made the road into the farm more difficult to access, trying to cut off the supplies and visitors crucial to the farm's success. By the time I arrived to visit, the road to the hilltop farm had been closed by the Israeli military a couple of kilometers out from the entrance. Getting to the farm therefore involved a hilly walk over terrain that was not always smooth. On the walk to the farm, I noticed the long downhill path on which we started our journey and made a mental note to be sure to be at the front of the group when we headed out, to get a head start on the long, slow incline back to the bus. On the trip back to the bus, I had to pause numerous times to catch my breath, but I made it back just fine. On top of being privileged to spend time with the Nassar family, who work tirelessly for peace and justice and the truth of God's call to love our neighbors and even our enemies, this was a moment of redemption for me. I was a fat woman in a country not my own, facing a bit of physical difficulty in service of seeking to love God and my neighbors, and my body did not stop me. My body asked for a bit of intentionality, care, and time, but my body served God just fine.

I don't know whether I responded that night in London to an authentic calling of the Holy Spirit or whether I made the decision out of the belief that I had no other option, that the only thing left for someone who could not summon the self-control to honor her temple into thinness was ministry in the United States—considered at the time to be equally valid to, if less glamorous than, international missions. I don't think that's a question I can ever fully answer. I believe that God has created me for a calling and that God is sovereign, but sometimes I wonder what path I would have taken if the church had not so adamantly insisted through structural bias and exclusion that one door was closed. Yet, that closed door has led me to a US-based ministry with the goal that there will be no more teenagers who believe their body makes them unqualified for any aspect of loving God and loving their neighbors.

Our fat bodies do not disqualify us from serving God or doing so effectively. Our bodies—fat or thin, toned or soft—are made in the image of God and equipped for every good work. Honoring the temple of our bodies means using our body in the ways it is uniquely equipped to love God and to love neighbors, not to shame ourselves into believing our fatness makes us unqualified to serve God. I see the validation of this truth most often in writings about the bodies of mothers—bodies that literally stretch and grow to accommodate life, bodies that put their own sleep, nutrition, and comfort aside in order to nurture a new life. Our culture has not always been this way, praising the stretch marks and sleepy eyes of those who nurture the young, but we have come to see the honor that comes with using our bodies, just as they are, in service of noble and holy pursuits.

Fat bodies deserve the same dignity. We can show up and be present at the bedsides of the sick, prepare food or clothing for those who are hungry and cold. We can honor the temple of our body—put in the service of God—in the many ways we are physically present in our community. This dignity does not change, no matter the limits on any person's body or movements. Those who struggle with painful disease or disabilities have a right to express their pain, to proclaim all the ways that their body does not feel good. Yet even bodies in pain are made in the image of God and are worthy of dignity and respect.

Yes, there are individual things we can do to care for our bodies; making wise and informed choices for our holistic health is a good thing. It is not, however, central to the gospel's call on our life. Those who live with chronic or debilitating illness, no matter the cause, are not excluded from being able to serve God and others. That service may look different within the limits of what someone's body or pain or mind will allow. We are not all required to serve in the same way. My mother has battled increasingly debilitating chronic illness most of my life. She is one of the most generous people I know. At Christmas, her table becomes an assembly line to put together small gifts for the staff at the local restaurants she and my dad frequent. If I hear of a need in our community (the foster-children clothes closet needs pajamas, a friend of a friend needs clothes, one of the local food pantries is out of a staple, etc.), she will often meet that need. My mother's illnesses are hard; they are painful. I wish, and she especially does, that she could live a life free of pain. The pain and disease in her body do not prevent her from living into the calling God has on her life to be generous to her neighbors.

BODIES AND TEMPLES

Perhaps the passage I have heard preached most often in regards to treating my body like a temple is 1 Corinthians 6:

> "All things are lawful for me," but not all things are helpful. "All things are lawful for me," but I will not be dominated by anything. "Food is

meant for the stomach and the stomach for food"—and God will destroy both one and the other. The body is not meant for sexual immorality, but for the Lord, and the Lord for the body. And God raised the Lord and will also raise us up by his power. Do you not know that your bodies are members of Christ? (1 Corinthians 6:12–15, ESV)

Here, the passage continues into a few-verse discussion on sexual immorality. Those verses are almost always skipped when this passage is preached. The reader often moves straight to verse 19: "Or do you not know that your body is a temple of the Holy Spirit within you, whom you have from God? You are not your own, for you were bought with a price. So glorify God in your body" (1 Corinthians 6:19–20, ESV).

I could not begin to count the number of times I have heard this passage preached as a message against fatness. It occurs so frequently that when I finally heard a preacher whose sermon on 1 Corinthians 6 included those middle verses and did not engage in body shame or make a quick and easy joke about fatness, I sent him a thank-you note for sticking to the context of sexual immorality and not fat-shaming in the process.

I have read various Bible commentaries on this passage, and I haven't found one that focuses on food, weight, physical health, or body size. They all focus on sexual immorality. Our cultural teachings about our bodies have infiltrated the way we speak about and read Scripture. Of course, it is good to think about our contemporary life and reality when we read Scripture, rather than just reading it as history, but we have let unhealthy ideas about body sneak into our sermons.

The oft-ignored middle of the 1 Corinthians 6 passage tells us what all of verses 12–20 are about: sexual immorality. Certainly this doesn't mean that we cannot apply this passage to other areas of understanding embodiment and the indwelling of the Holy Spirit, but it is wrong to use these verses as a weapon or a tool of body conformity. To avoid using these verses as support for dualistic thinking that makes the body the enemy of the soul, we must learn to read the verses in context. Rather than assuming we know what these verses mean based on our contemporary understanding of a disciplined body, we should examine the verses themselves to learn what it truly means to "glorify God in your body." While we can infer from the passage that our bodies are worthy of honor and holiness, proscribing a list of ways that we avoid "profaning" the body based on our current ideals is a mistake. Instead, we can read this passage in a way that serves as a reminder of the *imago Dei* present in our bodies.

Verse 13 at first seems to suggest that food and our hunger are evil and something that will pass away. The verse says, "'Food is meant for the stomach and the stomach for food'—and God will destroy both one and the other. The body is [meant] for the Lord, and the Lord for the body." Some commentators point out that "all things are lawful to me" and "food is meant for the stomach and the stomach for food" were common sayings in Corinth and suggest that Paul is using this nod to his cultural context to make his point. The latter phrase may indicate that the Corinthians believed that food and what was put in the body did not matter because eventually we all die. However, the talk of food and stomachs is just a way to get to the main point of this passage, which is addressing sexual immorality. The Corinthians may have used the food/stomach argument as a way to say that gratifying sexual desires is just as natural as eating.[1] The main argument Paul is making against sexual immorality is that it defiles the body, which is the temple of God. In other words, "The body does not exist merely to perform purely physical functions within the sphere of the natural world: *it is for the Lord.* . . . It exists in order that the human person may carry out the commands of Christ."[2] Sexual immorality can be an obstacle to fully serving God in our bodies, just as the food we consume can be when we are gluttonous.

Our understanding of sexual immorality, just like gluttony, is often more rooted in contemporary cultural ideas than in the radical call of Jesus. Sexual immorality is that which breaks community and dishonors the image of God in another person. Sexual immorality views our body as inconsequential. To use another's body in selfish sexual fulfillment is immoral. To prioritize the sexual appeal of a body above all else is immoral. Sex is not a sin, but it is possible to engage in sinful sexual acts and attitudes. Sexual purity cannot be narrowly defined as maintaining virginity until marriage. In the same way, body purity is not about the food in our body or the size of our thighs. The standard for measuring our faith practices is always the way in which our life is tuned in to our call to love God and love neighbors as ourselves. Without love, as the Scriptures say, we are nothing. No strict diet and exercise regimen or purity laws will get us there any faster.

Not only is the body for the Lord, but "the Lord is for the body" (1 Corinthians 6:13). God cares about our bodies, how they are treated and viewed. Heaping shame onto our bodies is certainly in opposition to a Lord who is for our bodies.

In a sermon on this passage from the early 1930s at Moody Memorial Church in Chicago (over twenty years before Charlie Shedd's *Pray Your Weight Away* ushered in the modern Devotional Diet industry), H. A. Ironside rightly warns of the dangers of elevating one's appetite or love of food to the level that it is a dangerous, life-controlling addiction. There are absolutely no connections to fatness or body size in his critique and warning, however. Ironside preaches against the dangers of living "to feed the belly."[3] He emphasizes that our spirit, soul, and flesh all belong to Christ, are all a member of Christ. "It is not merely as an aggregation of redeemed souls that the Church is the Body of Christ, but as men and women having physical constitutions we belong to Christ, and my body is to manifest the holiness of Christ, my body is to be used in devotion to Him."[4]

Understanding that our body is a temple and that God dwells in our body spurs us to treat our body (and others' bodies) with dignity. Fatness is considered undignified only if that is our cultural assumption. An understanding of body acceptance that honors the body as it is, rather than trying to make the body into something it is not, is a better way to show dignity to the temple that is the dwelling place of God. Dignity looks like eating to nourish our bodies, rather than a strict diet used as punishment. Dignity looks like joy in movement, rather than feeling as if we deserve to be in pain as punishment for pumpkin pie.

LIVING SACRIFICES

In high school, I had Romans 12:1–2 on the front of my school binders, hanging near my mirrors, and taped inside of my locker. I memorized it, reciting it over and over throughout my day in hopes that it would literally shape me. These verses say, "Therefore, I urge you, brothers and sisters, in view of God's mercy, to offer your bodies as a living sacrifice, holy and pleasing to God—this is your true and proper worship. Do not conform to the pattern of this world, but be transformed by the renewing of your mind. Then you will be able to test and approve what God's will is—his good, pleasing and perfect will" (NIV). It was my diet motivation as a teenager. I was convinced that sacrificing my body in a way that honored God meant that I needed to deny myself until I got thinner. Since my efforts never succeeded, the verse became an elusive goal, one that made me certain I was never truly worshipping God in my fat body.

In college, when I first started learning about fat acceptance and Health at Every Size, I actively avoided Romans 12 for a few years, certain I had failed and scared that I was abandoning sound Christian ethics.

Later, I read Romans 12 again, this time through the eyes of someone who had spent many years learning to accept my own body and to critique the ways in which the world and church had told me that my body was wrong. The first thing I noticed is that my body is described as "holy and pleasing" without any need for transformation, and it is the mind that is the subject of renewal. It is the mind that must be renewed to understand how God views our bodies that were lovingly created in the image of God, and to see that our bodies were deemed the perfect form for the incarnation of Christ.

Using Romans 12 to insist that we must sacrifice the pounds on our bodies in order to be "holy and acceptable" to God denies the truth that our bodies are already created in the image of God, already formed wonderfully. Our bodies matter and can be used to the glory of God. There is no indication in these verses that we need to change our bodies or make better ones in order for them to be acceptable as a living sacrifice. If the will of God that is to result in bodily sacrifice is simply that we are to eat more fiber and run around the block each day, then we have a very thin and selfish gospel. If this passage and others that speak of the importance of our bodies are simply about maintaining modern Western assumptions about our bodies, then we do a great disservice to the people who should have been helped by our commitment to putting our bodies into the act of service to God. Sacrificing our bodies means that we use our bodies for the greater body of Christ, to build community. Thin bodies do not make the love of God known to the world simply by nature of being thin. God does not require this of us.

To focus on whether or not our bodies are *pleasing* and *acceptable* to God when God deemed them so from the moment of creation is to distract Christians with an anxiety that consumes our minds at the expense of building community, serving others, and proclaiming the radical embodied love of Jesus Christ that is for all people. To do so is a sin and an obstacle to the kingdom of God. The Psalms tell us that our bodies are fearfully and wonderfully made, and that our Creator saw even our frame, our form, before it came to be. Nothing in Scripture suggests that God desires people to be thin or that thinness is the best form of the human body. Christians need to repent of the way in which we have co-opted secular ideals and biases in the name of "honoring God" and choose instead to seek to honor the worth and dignity of all humans.

Rather than being required to join in a never-ending quest for a perfect body, we are called not to conform our bodies to patterns of this world. We are justified, we are sanctified, just as we are. That is enough to present our physical bodies—our stretched-mark skin and dimply thighs—as a holy and acceptable offering to God.

NOTES

1. Margaret E. Thrall, *The Cambridge Bible Commentary on the New English Bible: I and II Corinthians* (Cambridge: Cambridge University Press, 1965), 46.

2. Thrall, *Cambridge Bible Commentary*, 47.

3. H. A. Ironside, *Addresses on the First Epistle to the Corinthians* (Neptune, NJ: Loizeaux Brothers, 1986), 193.

4. Ironside, *Addresses on the First Epistle to the Corinthians*, 194.

6

BUT WHAT ABOUT YOUR HEALTH?

I dread the process of finding a new doctor. My experience with doctors is mostly them telling me to lose weight, no matter if I came in for the flu or a physical. For many years, I just avoided the doctor, not wanting to subject myself to a lecture. During my years in Chicago, I needed a doctor to perform a work-mandated physical and was met with my first fat-positive doctor. She examined me and said, "You are the healthiest person I have seen all week." She became my primary-care physician, and for the first time in my life, if something in my body felt odd, I didn't just ignore it. I sought medical advice. I signed up for my annual physicals and had routine, preventive care.

When I moved back to Georgia, I was not expecting to get so lucky but made the appointment anyway. I parked the car in front of the office and glanced up to see weight-loss ads plastered on the windows facing the parking lot. Inside the office, weight-loss posters filled the walls, and diet commercials played in a loop on the waiting-room television. I double-checked to make sure I had located a standard primary-care practice for my annual physical, looking up the website on my phone first and then asking the receptionist, "This is just a regular doctor, right? She can do a routine annual physical?" She assured me I was in the correct place. I sat in the waiting room, rehearsing my responses should I find myself on the receiving end of unwanted weight-loss directives. I would ask the doctor to provide me with a peer-reviewed study showing an effective weight-loss program in which the majority of the participants lost a significant amount of weight and kept it off for more than five years. I knew she would not be able to provide such a study; none exists. There is no method.

Once in the exam room, the nurse took my blood pressure and said the reading was high, which was very out of the norm for me. The blood pressure cuff she used had really been too small for my arm, and I knew the size of the cuff—along with my anxiety about a new doctor and discomfort with the weight-loss ads—could raise my blood pressure, so I didn't think too much of it. When the doctor entered the exam room, she quickly mentioned my blood pressure and went straight into a discussion of beginning meds. I asked her to retake my blood pressure using a correct-size cuff. She left the room and returned a few minutes later, saying there was not one in the office. She dropped the discussion of the blood pressure medication. I was in an office that aggressively targeted itself as a weight-loss clinic (and thereby certainly wanted fat patients to make use of their services), and they did not have the correct medical equipment to diagnose fat patients. The doctor was willing to prescribe medication based on the reading of an inappropriate tool, a diagnosis the doctor gave up with only minimal pushback.

The longer the appointment went on, the more I knew that this was not my doctor. She asked me no questions about how I felt, what I ate, or my activity level. Yet she instructed me on what to cut out of my diet and told me to exercise more. At the time, I ate a mostly vegan diet and thoroughly enjoyed her look of shock and the few speechless moments it took her to recover when I told her about my food choices.

I began the search for a different local primary-care doctor and eventually found one who took a medical history and advises me on health based on lab work and my actual experience, rather than her assumptions based on my size.

I have spent years educating myself on fatness, bias, and health and now know enough to speak up when best medical practices are ignored and to keep looking for a doctor who sees *me* and not just their preconceived ideas about fat bodies. I lost only one frustrating afternoon and a copay. Many fat people in our country leave the first doctor's office feeling ashamed, holding an unnecessary prescription, and thinking they deserve to be treated as if they are stupid, lazy, and sick. We all deserve adequate, appropriate, evidence-based medical care.

I am generally in agreement with a philosophy called Health at Every Size (HAES), a movement that seeks to prioritize the health of every size of body without a focus on weight. The movement's website (haescommunity.com) says, "Health at Every Size® principles help us advance social justice, create an inclusive and respectful community, and support people of all sizes in finding compassionate ways to take care of themselves." The HAES name and much of the framework are from the book *Health at Every Size: The Surprising Truth about Your Weight*,[1] by Linda

Bacon, PhD, though the concept, research, and application of HAES have expanded beyond her book. Within this framework, HAES proponents recognize that weight changes may occur as people have declining or improving health, but that these weight changes are not universal norms or moral judgments. HAES uses a weight-neutral approach to fitness, nutrition, and health. The claim is not that all people are healthy, but that all people can work toward the goal of improved health.

This system of beliefs promotes healthful eating, physical activity, and routine and regular health care under the supervision of trained and qualified health care providers. This is a holistic approach that asks you to pay attention to your body (energy, strength, endurance, mood, aches and pains, etc.) and to use medical measurements (blood sugar and cholesterol levels, heart and kidney function, etc.) under the care of a physician to determine your health without using weight as the determining factor of whether you are healthy or not. In addition, HAES advocates for access to physical activities for people of all sizes and abilities: gym equipment should be able to handle six hundred pounds or more, athletic wear should be available in a wide range of sizes, and people should not be made to feel ashamed for moving and living in a fat body. Bodies of every size deserve access to adequate and appropriate medical care and the freedom to participate in a wide range of physical activities.

I support HAES but with this caution: we need to be sure that enthusiasm for health does not shift into *healthism*. Healthism is the prioritization of health to an extreme degree, where persons living with disease or disabilities find themselves to be second-class citizens. In this way of thinking, health becomes a moral obligation, and those who fail to pursue health become outcasts.

Often the Christian argument for weight loss, which we will discuss more in chapter 8, is that God desires the best for us and our bodies, and people assume that means good health. Since most people assume that you must be thin in order to be healthy, the argument that God wants us to be thin comes next. Certainly, the Bible is full of healing narratives; Jesus frequently heals people, especially those who suffer from conditions that ostracize them from their community—the blind beggar, the leper, the woman who bled for twelve years. Yet God does not always heal. The thorn in Paul's side could have been an illness of some sort. In 2 Samuel, we meet Mephibosheth, a son of Jonathan who cannot walk because of an injury he suffered as a child. King David welcomes him into his palace. Illness persists in our world, even among the faithful. Surely there is a place for persons living with illness or disability in the body of Christ—the church—and our communities, even though healing can sometimes happen.

We learn more about health every day, including unlearning lessons we thought we knew to be true. The definitions of healthful food and healthy bodies change frequently as we expand our knowledge, and there is often disagreement among professionals. Surely God does not require of us the pursuit of such a changing target in order for us to be deemed worthy of love and purpose.

Healthism often leads to expending extreme amounts of time and resources on the goal of health. So many of the latest diet fads require very specific menus and/or preparation methods. We measure portions into color-coded boxes, memorize food tables to count the points in our meals, stock up on expensive juices that promise to cleanse our body, and fill our carts with expensive (and often inaccessible) organic ingredients and produce. We moralize our food—calling broccoli "good" and chocolate "bad," and telling ourselves that eating a cupcake is "cheating." The goal, we say, is health, but our newsfeeds are full of people reporting on their weight loss or the ways their clothes are getting baggier once they started eating food they call "correct." Our obsession with the right kinds of food (gluten-free, hormone-free, dairy-free, whole grains, raw, vegan, organic, natural, local, etc.) only exacerbates things for those who are tempted to obsess about their food choices.

A related term is *orthorexia*. This is the extreme obsession with eating the "correct food" or behaving in the "correct way" in order to be healthy. One of the goals (or indicators of success) of healthism or orthorexia is often a slim body. Although HAES does not advocate for a slim body, there is still danger of falling into a healthism trap with a HAES framework by setting up a good-fat-person–versus–bad-fat-person competition. (In the fat acceptance community this is commonly referred to as the good fatty vs. bad fatty dichotomy.) This creates a hierarchy in which fat people who eat vegetables or go biking are good at being fat and worthy of some acceptance, while those who drive everywhere and eat frozen dinners are somehow bad at being fat and less worthy of dignity and respect. Even if some people intentionally choose fast food and a sedentary lifestyle, they do not become less human, less worthy of respect, or lose the image of God or the presence of the Holy Spirit inside of them. This remains true even if those choices make them aesthetically unappealing to the normative gaze of our culture or increase their chances of dying before the average age.

A few years ago, I was walking through the grocery store and had a sudden intense pain in my side. I felt light-headed and nauseated. The onset was sudden and sharp enough that I went to an urgent-care clinic, where the doctor diagnosed me with a raging kidney infection. *Raging* was the doctor's term. (This doctor, I should note, was excellent in terms of treating my symptoms and not my size.) I took antibiotics for a couple of weeks and scheduled a follow-up to make sure my kidney was okay. I became acutely aware of where my kidney is located in my body, thanks to the severe pain that popped up a couple of times a day for the next week or so. Every time I tried to sneeze, my recovering kidney painfully protested and shut it down in a move of self-preservation. The kidney won the involuntary muscle contest inside my body. I did not sneeze for a week.

This was the beginning of more frequent trips to the doctor in my life. The infection was likely the result of an untreated infection elsewhere, and I had had no symptoms before my sudden pain and nausea in the grocery store. So we needed to figure out what my body wasn't telling me. My primary-care doctor wanted me to have an MRI to make sure the kidney looked okay. The nurse at the imaging clinic handed me a size extra-large pair of scrub pants to wear into the machine. I told her I would need a bigger pair. She dug around for a while before she produced a size XXL and said, "These are probably too big, but they should work!" I am not quite sure if she actually thought that XXL pants would be too big for me, or if she was performing some social ritual in which she tries to compliment me by suggesting that my body is not a size XXL, despite all visual evidence to the contrary. When clothing is sized generously, I might be able to wear a 2X, but a 4X is what actually fits me most of the time. I mentioned the need for larger clothing to the nurse who had handed me the pants. She shrugged it off, remarking, "Oh, well, laundry gets delivered tomorrow."

I managed to squeeze into the XXL pants and was grateful I was allowed to leave my own shirt on. I exited the changing room and walked around the corner to wait my turn for the MRI machine, with my legs and lower abdomen crammed into the pants. It was humiliating. I wanted to be invisible. I felt as if my body was too much in that moment: too much for the pants, too much for health, too much me. I felt hyper-visible; I longed for flowing clothes that draped and hid my body. At the same time, I wanted to embrace my hyper-visibility. I wanted all of the staff to see me crammed ridiculously into the pants.

It was not my fault the pants did not fit; they did not have adequate supplies. They should see and notice and fix. I wanted the people around me who had the power to influence the size of the clothing stocked in the office to see and be embarrassed that their facility was so poorly equipped. I doubt they noticed. I'm glad I spoke up. Thankfully, the MRI machine itself was able to accommodate my body even while the clothing was inadequate. I cannot imagine I am the only person of my size or the largest person ever to need their services. Yet, again, a medical facility had failed to have adequate tools to accommodate my body.

A few months later, my primary-care physician diagnosed me with diabetes and hypertension. I have preached the dangers of healthism for years; now my conviction to the truth that all bodies are good bodies was tested. In contrast to the doctor I had seen over a year prior, who abandoned her hypertension diagnosis when I asked for the correct medical equipment, this doctor had the correct-size cuff, ran full panels of my blood work, and took a complete medical history. Meds were prescribed only after all of those things were completed and reviewed. Perhaps my blood pressure had truly been high at the doctor eighteen months prior, but that doctor had decided I was not worth the hassle when

I pushed back to make sure I was being treated correctly. My fat body did not get adequate health care.

With my diagnoses came medications, some changes to my food and movement habits, and a lot of shame and questions as I worked to wrap my brain around being fat and sick. I had said for years that one did not need to be healthy to have value—that fat people did not need to be healthy to be good. My public life as a fat-acceptance advocate was just getting started. The kidney infection hit as hundreds of comments came in on an article I wrote for *Christianity Today*, titled "God Loves My Fat Body as It Is."[2] The commenters frequently told me that I would die because of my weight, a common response to the work of fat-acceptance advocates. (I always feel the need to remind them that thinness does not grant us immortality.) In the first few weeks after my diabetes diagnosis, while I learned the routine of checking my blood sugar and paying attention to how late at night I ate to control overnight glucose levels, I stood on a stage and told a crowd of people about the freedom I had found to accept my fat body. I realized that as much as I rejected the good-fat–versus–bad-fat dichotomy, I still had some pride about being the good fat. My health had been a way I could justify to people that they should listen to me.

I messaged a friend who had been among the first

to introduce me to fat acceptance, to let her know about my diagnosis. I shared with her my fears about no longer being a "good" fat person, but also anxieties I had that the changes I made to control my blood sugar levels would cause me to become thin. She, rightly, assured me that the chances that any changes I would make would take me from a size 26 to a size 6 were slim. If my body was going to become thin after a few changes to my food and exercise, it would have happened during one of my countless attempts before. The idea I would lose a significant amount of weight was a bit of wishful thinking—that maybe disease management was finally the diet that would work to transform me.

Realizing that I still found myself desiring thinness was one more anxiety that came with the diagnosis. The benefits of thinness are everywhere around me. Clothes are easier to find. Airline seats are easier to navigate. Relationships seem to come easier. If I was thin, I wouldn't have to worry whether I would fit in the booth at the restaurant. I could sit down on a friend's patio chair without worrying whether it would crush under my weight. I could finally try out kayaking without having to track down an expensive kayak that would withstand my weight without sinking. The world is built for people under 250 pounds, and I don't lose any fat-acceptance honesty points to occasionally feel the desire to be in that easily accessible world.

FAT ACCEPTANCE

The fat-acceptance (FA) movement says that all people—regardless of size or their health or how flattering their manner of dress or how well they perform standards of acceptability—deserve to be treated with respect and dignity. The FA movement often explicitly rejects any call to prove the health of a fat person. A human is a human, and the health of a fat human does not determine whether or not that person should be able to exist in public without mockery. Those who speak mainly from a FA viewpoint are not anti-health, but health does not have a primary place in the discussion. This movement advocates for various rights for fat people, such as demanding that medical facilities have appropriate equipment for fat bodies. The FA movement is known for its efforts to make fat people visible in a world that would rather not have to see fat bodies. Short hairstyles (that are deemed not good for a fat face), body art, and clothing choices that people say are only acceptable on thin bodies (crop tops, tight-fitting clothes, etc.) are common.

Every body is allowed to be active and look however the body looks in the process. On a group hike,
I paused to look at a small creek and catch my breath.
A child next to me stared for a few moments at my
fat arm, visible on a rare day I wore a sleeveless top.
She poked my arm and said, "You need to exercise."
I looked at her and smiled, "That's exactly what we
are doing! But that doesn't mean my arm will look
different later. Bodies come in all sizes, no matter
what activities they do." I enjoy the opportunity to
push back on cultural messages when I respond to
children's curiosity about my body. I knew her par-
ents, who weren't in earshot, would back me up and
be glad I gave that answer. Every body is allowed
to go hiking through hilly forests and to bare arms
in the heat of a Georgia summer. We do not need
to achieve a "hiking body," whatever that is, before
we are allowed to enjoy physical activity. We do not
have to punish ourselves on gym equipment during
the off-hours, when people aren't likely to see us,
before we are allowed to show up and be visible.
More than that, you are allowed to wear a sleeveless
crop top while sitting in public, eating ice cream.
Your body, no matter how fat it is, does not disqualify you from enjoying life.

ANTI-FAT BIAS

Anti-fat bias has very real implications for the holistic health of fat bodies in ways that have nothing to do with our size. A study of professionals who treat eating disorders found that those "with stronger weight bias were more likely to attribute obesity to behavioral causes, express more negative attitudes and frustrations about treating obese patients, and perceive poorer treatment outcomes for these patients."[3] Nursing and psychology students who exhibit signs of anti-fat bias are in danger of providing poor quality of care to their patients, especially their female ones.[4] In another study, treatment of an obese patient, relative to treatment of a non-obese patient, showed "more negative stereotyping, less anticipated patient adherence, worse perceived health, more responsibility attributed for potentially weight-related presenting complaints and less visual contact directed toward the obese . . . patient."[5] People can often sense when someone thinks poorly of them, and feeling that way in the presence of a doctor only increases shame. When studies show that even those being trained in the field of nutrition, medicine, and health maintain a fat bias, it is evidence of the numerous walls of oppression fat people must overcome in order to be treated equally.

Thankfully, studies have shown that some of this weight bias can be mitigated with relatively small changes. Medical students who receive training on the multiple causes of obesity and on anti-fat discrimination show a reduction in anti-fat bias.[6] A study published in 2014 in *Health Psychology* shows that if we reduce (and eliminate) the negative media portrayals of fat people, we can greatly reduce the anti-fat bias in the greater population.

When I speak to groups about fatness, I often begin by asking them to tell me the stereotypes of fat people. Usually, there are a few brave volunteers who will get the ball rolling and call out things we aren't supposed to say in polite company, especially not when there's a fat woman standing in front of you. They call out words like lazy, stupid, unathletic, undisciplined, poor, uneducated, sick, jolly, funny, pretty face, and a good personality. These same words are used whether the people answering are Christians or not. For Christians, the way we talk about what it means to honor our bodies influences our assumptions about fat bodies. The prevailing narrative in the church is that we honor our bodies, our temples, by making them thin (and presumably healthy). This theology is influential.

These are more than just words. These are beliefs that influence actions. These are beliefs held by people who decide who gets a job, who gets housing, who makes what grade on an assignment, who gets a chance to excel. These are beliefs held by people who are charged with caring for someone's mental or physical health, beliefs held by architects and clothing designers. These are the words that are associated with fat people inside the minds of people who produce entertainment and people who decide how much space there is in your airline seat. Beliefs lead to actions that have consequences for everything from how comfortable someone is in the world to whether or not they get fair and unbiased health care.

I once volunteered for a Christian conference about justice. As part of the deal, we got a free volunteer T-shirt. I typically don't even bother to expect a free T-shirt that is actually of any use to me, because they often stop ordering at XL, sometimes 2X. I have been the solo person without the group T-shirt more times than I can count in my life. However, this conference requested T-shirt size early, so that they could order the correct sizes. I replied with my T-shirt size (4X) and thanked them profusely for asking up front, because it meant I would be included, that I would look like I belonged on the volunteer team. The weekend of the conference came, and I showed up a day early to do the pre-volunteer work. When I went to pick up the T-shirt to wear as I volunteered the next two days, the largest size they had in women's was an XL. I mentioned this to a staff person, thinking perhaps they had put mine to the side. They looked perplexed and directed me to the men's T-shirt section, where I was given a men's 2X. This was doable but still did not fit well. It was tight and uncomfortable. On top of that, the men's and women's shirts had different designs. I looked different again. The disappointment at being excluded from the group because of my size was intensified because of the hope I'd had for a different experience.

Groups that don't have the ability to preorder shirts in as-needed sizes should order sizes all the way up to at least 6X—larger if your community needs it. If the T-shirt (or choir robe) company doesn't make shirts in size 6X, get a better T-shirt company. (Companies will often charge more for plus-size shirts than other shirts; do not pass on that cost. Just divide to find the average cost of a shirt, and let every adult pay the same price.) A couple of years after my experience with the T-shirt at the conference, my church was ordering T-shirts. The woman in charge of it made sure that the shirts went up to my size, and I was forever grateful. It turned out that the color I wanted (pink) didn't come in the size I needed (I can only assume because the company decided both that no woman would be that large and that only women wear pink). However, the T-shirt order came in a variety of colors, and no color was designated as only for a specific gender. I simply chose another color, and my angst was with the limits of the T-shirt company, rather than with my church.

Shopping outside of conference and group T-shirts is no easier for fat people. If a store you love carries your size but their clothing sizes stop at 2X or 3X, ask the store to carry larger sizes. Some stores carry their plus-size clothing only online, meaning plus-size people must spend extra on shipping and not have the opportunity to try on clothes before purchasing them. I recently walked into a new-to-my-area plus-size store. I knew that online this retailer carried sizes up to 6X, and I was excited for a new place to shop. The vast majority of clothes in stock only went up to a 2X. There were a handful of 3Xs and 4Xs, two or three 5Xs, and no 6Xs in the store. I asked, and the salesperson said they only carry those online. Even in a space that is supposed to be about my body, I find I am excluded from participating. If the clothes ordered online don't fit, we are out the original shipping price plus the return shipping price. When you consider the intersections of fatness and poverty, clothing becomes another justice issue. God literally calls us to clothe the naked. When there are no stores in which to acquire clothing for a person's body, then a faithful response is to step up and demand more. A good way to test your access to clothing is to ask yourself, "If I spill coffee all over my white dress shirt thirty minutes before an important meeting, can I find a replacement shirt that fits me in a store nearby?" For me, the answer is no, unless I happen to be next door to a plus-size clothing store like Lane Bryant.

It's not just about difficulty in finding a T-shirt. The exploitation and oppression of fat bodies is prevalent in our culture. If we as the church are to love our neighbors (as we love ourselves), we must understand that honoring our bodies is not the same thing as being thin. That belief fuels anti-fat bigotry that encourages structural sin in our culture that harms fat bodies. While a mainstream body-positive movement has picked up steam in the past few years, fat people still face discrimination on multiple fronts.

Any person who has been a fat child in elementary school understands that fat bias from childhood peers can mean poor emotional health and prevents kids from doing things like playing with others on the playground. It's an ironic, heartbreaking consequence that the result of so much anti-fat bias is for fat people to avoid physical activity. Anecdotal stories abound, but there is a growing amount of scholarly research on the issue of discrimination against fat people. On top of schoolyard bullying, fat children face increasing pressures from authorities in their lives to be thin. In 2012, Children's Healthcare of Atlanta (CHOA) began an ad campaign targeting childhood obesity that included billboards with pictures of fat children, frowning, with captions such as "Warning: It's hard to be a little girl if you're not."[7] In a commercial from the same ad campaign, a young fat girl says, "I don't like to go to school because all the other kids pick on me. It hurts my feelings." Then the screen turns black, and the caption tells us, "Being fat takes the fun out of being a kid."[8] Instead of addressing bullying, these ads blame the fat child for her own abuse. The American Academy of Pediatrics reports that the rate of eating disorders in children under the age of twelve rose 119 percent between 1999 and 2006.[9] Our idolatry of thinness is ruining the lives of children.

The consequences for being fat in the world continue to grow more and more serious as the discrimination continues in systematic and subconscious ways. A study published in the *American Journal of Obesity Research* found that "clear and consistent stigmatization, and in some cases discrimination, can be documented in three important areas of living: employment, education, and health care."[10] The research also indicates that there is the likelihood of "discrimination occurring in adoption proceedings, jury selection, housing, and other areas."[11] The very basic expectations that people have about life—housing, family, education, and a job—are all affected by the often-subconscious biases about fat people. The assumption is that fat people can be slim if they exercise and manage their diet. This assumption could lead a hiring manager to assume that a fat person has no willpower or has some moral or character flaw.

Perhaps most ironically, as my own experience illustrates, fat bias exists even among health, nutrition, and medical professionals. This is a significant barrier to fat people being able to obtain fair, equitable, and appropriate medical care.[12]

There are also physical barriers. A fat person moving about this world encounters numerous roadblocks in their day-to-day life, which we navigate around in order to live. In my life, something as simple as finding a seat can be a multi-variable maneuver. If I enter a new room, I immediately scan the type of furniture and the placement of the furniture. I am eyeballing a path that is wide enough to allow me to move to my seat comfortably. I typically plan to stay seated until the event is over, even if the event does not call for it. Getting up and navigating my way through the chairs and people to use the restroom, check a phone message, step out for air, or speak to a friend across the room will bring attention to myself and my size as I squeeze and push my way through the narrow maze of chairs, tables, and humans. Even as a person who accepts and loves my own fat body, I have no desire to be a distracting spectacle to others, especially if I am in the midst of an event where the attention should not be on me, regardless of my size. At times, like when the pants I needed to wear for the MRI didn't fit, I am okay with (and can even be excited about) people seeing the way my body fits, or doesn't, into a space, in hopes that it will motivate them to action. Other times, I just want to be a person at a conference who can get to and from her seat easily—who isn't there to educate the world on the need for size-accessible spaces.

At Wild Goose Festival—a Christian art, spirituality, and music festival where a few thousand people camp for a long weekend—people carry their own chairs around. Camp chairs get slung over shoulders and popped open in front of stages, by tents, or just on the side of the path when someone wants to sit. There are some standard folding chairs available for people, but it is common for people to have their own as well. I love this. I get to carry a chair that is comfortable for me and sufficient for my body, and I don't stand out. I get to blend into the background. I walked into a session late once and decided I would just sit in one of the provided folding chairs, rather than disrupt the speakers by unfolding my camp chair. That seat hurt. The metal bars on the back corners dug into each side of my hips and left bruises.

Most places, I don't carry my own chair. I am always hoping for an armless chair. Arms on chairs prescribe the width of space I am allowed, and it is sure to be too narrow. I do a little dance for joy when I walk into a classroom, auditorium, or sanctuary that has wide, sturdy chairs with no arms and desks or tables that are separate pieces of furniture. Today I know how to both look for good seating options and speak up for myself when necessary, but if accommodations need to be made, there is still a moment of embarrassment, as I must make my body super visible to the people in charge of the space. As a child, teen, and young adult, I did not know to ask for seating that would not cause me to be distracted or in pain. I spent many uncomfortable years in small student desks with attached chairs. I was embarrassed by my need for a different seat. I assumed it was just another reason I needed to finally figure out how to change my body to literally fit in.

These inequalities in jobs, medical access and care, having an acceptable place to sit, and many others all exist despite the fact that there is a reported obesity epidemic. One would think that if the average size of a person in the United States is getting larger, or at least more diverse, then society would adjust to accommodate for those sizes. Instead, fat people are frequently told to change their bodies to fit into a society that privileges people who meet the culturally acceptable definitions of average.

I have to think about seating any time I am in a room with other people—church, theaters, classrooms, events. This has an impact on my education, my religious practice, my social life, and my entertainment options. And that's just getting to my seat.

The church Jesus tells us about is radically different. There is space for everyone. There is room for everyone to join the table, to have a seat. Being intentional to notice the ways we exclude fat bodies in our spheres of influence and seeking to widen those spaces is part of the way we love God and love others.[13] I dream of a community where people of all sizes and abilities are in the pews and leading from the front. I dream of a world where the choir robes and camp T-shirts fit everyone. In Scripture, we are told that every tongue and people will gather around the throne of God in heaven. I believe that includes every size. And I want that kingdom here on earth, where people—no matter their health or size or ability—are equipped to love and serve their neighbors and are supported in God's call on their life.

NOTES

1. Linda Bacon, *Health at Every Size: The Surprising Truth about Your Weight* (Dallas: Benbella, 2008).

2. J. Nicole Morgan, "God Loves My Fat Body as It Is," *Christianity Today*, October 14, 2015, https://tinyurl.com/y7a9ba5j.

3. Rebecca M. Puhl et al., "Weight Bias among Professionals Treating Eating Disorders: Attitudes about Treatment and Perceived Patient Outcomes," *International Journal of Eating Disorders* 47, no. 1 (January 2014): 65–75.

4. Tabitha Waller, Claudia Lampman, and Gwen Lupfer-Johnson, "Assessing Bias against Overweight Individuals among Nursing and Psychology Students: An Implicit

Association Test," *Journal of Clinical Nursing* 21, no. 23/24 (December 2012): 3504–12.

5. S. Persky and C. P. Eccleston, "Medical Student Bias and Care Recommendations for an Obese versus Non-obese Virtual Patient," *International Journal of Obesity* 35, no. 5 (May 2011): 728–35.

6. Phillippa C. Diedrichs and Fiona Kate Barlow, "How to Lose Weight Bias Fast! Evaluating a Brief Anti–Weight Bias Intervention," *British Journal of Health Psychology* 16, no. 4 (November 2011): 846–61.

7. Kathy Lohr, "Controversy Swirls around Harsh Anti-obesity Ads," NPR, January 9, 2012, https://tinyurl.com/ybqql469.

8. "TV Ad Targets Childhood Obesity," *ABC News*, January 2, 2012, https://tinyurl.com/6vzja6g.

9. D. S. Rosen, "Clinical Report—Identification and Management of Eating Disorders in Children and Adolescents," *Pediatrics* 126, no. 6 (December 2010): 1240–53.

10. Rebecca Puhl and K. D. Brownell, "Bias, Discrimination, and Obesity," *Obesity Research* 9 (2001): 788–805.

11. Puhl and Brownell, "Bias, Discrimination, and Obesity."

12. Mary Forhan and Salas Ximena Ramos, "Inequities in Healthcare: A Review of Bias and Discrimination in

Obesity Treatment," *Canadian Journal of Diabetes* 37, no. 3 (June 2013): 205–9.

13. Chapter 11 offers some practical tips and ideas for being a fat-positive community.

7

DIET
DEVOTIONALS

A scale stood in the corner of my sixth-grade Sunday school classroom. A tall metal column extended up from the base and led to a horizontal bar with weights you moved back and forth until it balanced out. This was not a small bathroom scale that could be pushed out of the way. It was the kind I stood on when I went to the doctor's office. (I remember the first time the nurse moved the large weight to 150 and began to slide the small one across the upper bar, seeing how many pounds she would add to 150 to get my weight. She went all the way to the end and had to move the larger weight to 200 and start the process over again. I passed 200 pounds in high school. As a sixth-grader, I had not yet seen my weight inch above 200, but I knew well the anxiety of standing on the scale with the numbers at eye level as the nurse's hand slid the weights back and forth while I wondered what number would finally balance the bar. Even as a child, I frequently heard from my doctor that I was too much.) We didn't use the scale in class, and I never remember it even being mentioned. It was there for the First Place class, a weight-loss-centered Bible study, which was held in that room on another day of the week. I knew it was for the class, because the church bulletin advertised it each week and it was mentioned from the pulpit.

Each Sunday, I'd walk into my classroom with my Bible in hand and would take a wary glance at the corner to find the tall metal object of judgment there, reminding me that I was fat. The metal folding chair I sat in each Sunday would squeak just a bit to echo the judgment I felt from the scale. I'd try to minimize the size of my body with legs crossed at the ankles and arms crossed on my lap in an effort to hide the roll of my stomach. Each week as I joined my class to read Bible stories and talk about what it means to love God, I was hyper-aware of that scale and what it meant about me, my body, and my faith.

First Place began in 1981 as a ministry of Houston's First Baptist Church. Beth Moore, a popular Christian Bible study author and teacher, endorsed the program in 2001 saying, "I joyfully testify to the biblical integrity of the Frist Place program. . . . God's way has worked for Carole, it has worked for me, and it will work for you!"[1] Often people don't believe me when I tell them that faith-based weight loss programs exist, or they assume it is a fringe market that no one really pays attention to. The truth is that there are many Christian weight-loss books, and Christians across the spectrum praise and promote their message. The "About" page of the First Place website (www.firstplace4health.com) states, "The tremendous success of First Place 4 Health is due to its biblical approach to weight loss and overall health management, which puts Christ first and improves every area of a person's life. This Christian weight-loss and healthy living program has guided hundreds of thousands of people to a healthy lifestyle and a closer walk with the Lord." For the proponents of First Place, a healthy lifestyle equals weight loss.

Carole Lewis, creator of First Place and coauthor of the book by the same name writes in the introduction to the 2008 edition: "Being overweight is often the warning sign that we are not where we need to be in life."[2] She says multiple times that the book is not just about weight loss but about giving our lives over to God. The book argues that losing weight is a side effect of a healthy, God-centered life. In a study on the program, researcher Lynne

Gerber discovered that First Place allows a variety of "measures of success": participants can achieve a desired body mass index (BMI); lose 10 percent of their original body weight; maintain their current weight; achieve a better number on a health indicator such as cholesterol or blood sugar; or simply do better on one of the spiritual goals of the program, such as Scripture memorization or regular prayer time.[3] While this may seem like a generous way to allow everyone to succeed, it also allows for advertising the "success" of a weight loss program when in reality there may be very little weight loss.

These types of misleading success stories build upon the myth that other, more disciplined people are achieving the physical and spiritual accomplishments of being self-controlled enough to have marked change in their bodies. But because this is not what is actually happening, the members of congregations where these devotional diets are used and promoted are being constantly told that they can achieve something unachievable, and if they do not achieve it, that the fault lies in their own lack of spiritual rigor, rather than in the program. In addition, Lewis places the fault for failure on the participants themselves. One of the ways the program measures success is by counting the number of times people show up for the weekly meetings. Lewis says, "Some people refuse to be accountable to the group after they have joined. If that occurs, it means they may also have a problem with accountability to God. . . . I have found that these people tend to refuse any sort of accountability."[4] *Accountability* is a Christian buzzword. In the faith tradition in which I was raised, having accountability meant you met regularly with other Christians in order to make sure you were living a faithful life. It was in your accountability group that you confessed your struggles, prayed for needs, and shared victories. It was understood that willingness to be accountable was essential to a healthy Christian faith. Lewis is effectively saying that a person who fails her program is failing as a Christian.

Here are some ways God tells us we can know if we are in line with God's call on our life: we love each other (John 13:35); we are so full of hope and faith and love that it's as if we are wearing it (1 Thessalonians 5:8); and others see in our lives the fruit of the Holy Spirit—love, joy, peace, patience, kindness, goodness, faithfulness, gentleness, and self-control (Galatians 5:22). (And self-control does not equal being thin. There are a variety of ways you can measure self-control; a scale is not needed!) God's measures for our growth and maturity as people of faith are wrapped up in how we exist in this world

133

in relation to those around us. When our days are consumed with counting nutritional components of food and monitoring the fluctuating numbers on a scale, we have even less time to consider how we might show more gentleness and patience to ourselves, much less our neighbors or enemies.

FOOD MORALIZATION AND DIET DEVOTIONALS

Our culture is so used to the moralization of food and bodies that equating treats to some type of sinful behavior is common. In 2012, Heather Bauer, a dietitian, published *Bread Is the Devil: Win the Weight Loss Battle by Taking Control of Your Diet Demons.*[5] The inside flap of the book explains that "bread is the devil" because of the "inevitable, demonic pull that certain bad habits exert on people who try to change their eating routines to drop the pounds."[6] The back jacket has an author picture showing Bauer to be very slim, blonde, and white—one more example of a person in a position of power (displaying socially endorsed standards of beauty and health) speaking on a topic that further marginalizes people on the outside. According to this book, those who succumb to their "hellish cravings" and enjoy the basket of bread when out to dinner find themselves "in the seventh circle of hell—the one reserved for glut-tons."[7] Once you get past the inside flap, the first sentence you are met with in the book is "Let's face it, everyone knows what goes into losing weight—it's all about eating less and exercising more, right?"[8] A brief look into the science of weight quickly shows that Bauer's premise is faulty; the simple formula of calories in, calories out doesn't reflect the complexity of the science of body size. But, her goal is to sell books by promising to get people thin.

Typically, the people who pick up diet books are looking for some solution to what they consider a problem in their life. Such people are presumably in a state of confusion or despair because their body size is a point of shame, frustration, and social discrimination. And the author is saying such people are under the control of demons and headed for hell, and that the way to lose weight is "simple"; they just lack the intelligence and/or discipline to make the simple magic formula work. All this on page 1.

A diet devotional is a book or program that uses faith-based reasoning or motivation to encourage people to lose weight. Bauer's book is not a diet devotional, but it utilizes the common social assumption that our food choices and our body size are connected to moral and religious judgments. I believe Bauer is being hyperbolic—that she doesn't actually think bread is the devil. Nevertheless, the comparison, in light of the way our culture equates thinness and godliness, is striking. Of course, even while Bauer's book makes our moral assumptions about food and body size explicit, it is not doing anything new. While Bauer may not be trying to make a legitimate faith-based claim, there are many who do.

The very first of the contemporary diet devotionals came in 1957, when Charles (Charlie) W. Shedd wrote *Pray Your Weight Away: How One Man Found the Help He Needed for the Greatest Act of Self-Discipline of His Life.* (I can assure you, weight does not pray away; if it did, there would be far fewer fat Christians.) This book is often cited as the beginning of the devotional-diet industry. Shedd was born in 1915 and spent fifty years of his life as a Presbyterian minister.[9] He wrote numerous books, including *Devotions for Dieters* (1983) and *The Fat Is in Your Head: A Lifestyle to Keep It Off* (1972). Other books were on various topics of day-to-day living as a Christian—marriage, family, finances, and so on.

Shedd wrote *Pray Your Weight Away* after losing one hundred pounds. He records in the book that his weight gain was intentional after he heard a physician say, "Fat people seldom die of TB" after tuberculosis took the life of his brother.[10] The back cover of this 1957 book shows a contemporary picture of Shedd and then a smaller picture of him that is captioned "three years and one hundred pounds ago."[11] On the inside jacket cover, we learn that Shedd tried for "fifteen years . . . to take off the surplus blubber which made him look like a small edition of Moby Dick.[12] The use of terms like "blubber" and "Moby Dick" is dehumanizing. When I lived in the shame of my fatness, I often questioned how I could exist—how the grotesque curves of my body could exist on the human form. I felt abnormal and did not see myself as fully human, or at least not the right kind of human. Shedd was never successful in his early weight loss goals. One day he began to view "reducing as a spiritual problem, and suggest[ed] a technique which may provide, for those who have faith, the power to heal the disease of obesity, permanently."[13] Shedd lost weight, decided this was divine affirmation that it was the path for all who desired to be slimmer, and wrote his book.

From the moment we take even the quickest glance at the book, we learn that fat is not just something that we may not like about ourselves or that we believe may be a problem for others, but that fat is a spiritual problem—a sin. Shedd says, "The fat you carry couldn't be within God's plan for you."[14]

The truth is that fat people are created in the image of God. We are human, no matter our body's form or our behavior or our choices. To suggest otherwise is abusive manipulation that attempts to marginalize people because of their size. The fact that Shedd himself experienced part of his life as a fat person does not make him immune to perpetuating this shame and abuse on others.

It is spiritually irresponsible to suggest there is any formula for faith. The things that sound like formulas in the Bible are not much help either. I am pretty confident that my faith could be measured at least as big as a mustard seed, and I have not yet made a mountain jump, despite my best attempts as a child (when my faith was probably a bit more pure and certainly far less complicated). Yet, the jacket summary of Shedd's book sets up the expectation that true Christians ("those that have faith") will be able to replicate Shedd's weight loss. In his argument, if you fail to reduce permanently, then perhaps you have a spiritual problem.

Along with trying to make actual mountains jump with my prayers as a child, I spent a good amount of time in my adolescence trying to understand why my faith didn't seem to be big enough for the mountain of my flesh to budge just a bit and move off my frame. I imagine this is a common thought for the faithful and fat. Shedd opens his book with the mustard seed reference in Matthew 17:20. He recounts

his prayer when he weighed three hundred pounds:
"Lord, there's a mountain of flesh on me. I've been
trying to move it ever since I was a boy. . . . Today I
say to this mountain, 'Get moving.' . . . I'm turning
my body over to you once and for all. . . . From this
day on I'll eat what *You* tell me to eat and live the way
You want me to live."[15]

Shedd has made his weight-loss goal a spiritual
goal. Failure means lack of faith. While he tells God
that he will eat and live the way God wants him to,
he implies that eating and living the way God wants
him to do so will result in a thinner body, a body
that does not invite ridicule or apathy. The logic is
this: if our bodies fail to conform, then perhaps we
did not listen well enough to what God said. And so
we never question our goals or what might actually
be happening in our bodies, we simply cycle through
diet after diet, beating ourselves up for not being
able to find enough self-discipline to make ourselves
acceptable to God. A 1958 review of Shedd's book is
sarcastic, noting that thanks to Shedd's explanation
of thinness being godly, the author "can now spot
those who have been elected from the foundation of
the world and can ask those lean, hungry, cadaver-
ous figures to pray for [him]."[16]

I firmly believe that the message God has for us is
this: "You are already enough. And, you are not too

much." Rather than all-consuming quests to reduce the size or our body because we believe that is what God wants, we can instead turn our focus to what God actually asks of us: to walk humbly, to love mercy, and to do justly. God does not require—or delight in—empty and routine sacrifices that fulfill the demands of the customs of this world (Micah 6). We do not need to throw our bodies onto an altar to be consumed. We *are* called to love God and to love neighbor and even enemies in the body we have.

Since giving up the quest for weight loss, my life has been enriched by the freedom to pursue God and live with purpose and intentionality. Losing weight is time-consuming. More significantly, it is mind-consuming. Every step—every bite—is considered and agonized over. Each morning begins with a step on the scale to see how strong your faith was the day before. You avoid buying new clothes because you are sure it is a waste of money; they will be too big soon, if all goes according to plan. So you avoid living a life that requires a wardrobe you refuse to buy. Dieting is no way to live. When I stopped dieting, I got my life back. Hours of meal planning turned into a much simpler grocery list; my time was free for something else. The morning check on the scale was gone, and I was free to focus on whatever activity the day held, without starting in shame.

There are certainly ways we can honor (or dishonor) God in our consumption and our choices with our bodies, as we saw in the chapter on gluttony. Faithful choices move us not toward a slimmer body, but toward holistic community with each other and creation.

I read Shedd's book while I was in seminary and working on a paper about the history of diet devotionals. It is long out of print, and I hunted down one copy through the wonders of interlibrary loan. I read it with a mixture of shock and recognition. In 1957, Shedd wasn't so worried about using polite words about fatness, and the things he wrote were blunt and echoed so many of my thoughts from the years when I still hated my body. I had long known that the church was a primary source of my shame about my body, especially in the way it had failed to affirm the image of God inside of me. To see it so explicitly in a book from a generation before mine confirmed I was not imagining the way the church contributed to my body shame. Lies about our bodies and what God thinks of them go so deep into Christianity that many of us view them as undebatable truth.

Shedd writes, reminding me of what was once my own insecurity, "Being fat means we wear a big sign on our neck that says 'insecurity!'—we cannot be confident people if we are fat. The confident seem to work as if the winds of the universe were at their back. But even the most effective air currents cannot move our hulking mass."[17] If Shedd is going to insist on dehumanizing fat bodies by referring to them as whales or inanimate "hulking masses," he could at least stick to the metaphor. While air may not move whales gracefully across the earth, water certainly carries them with beauty. And the hulking mass and strength of an elephant moving across the land is actually rather impressive and majestic. We can find grace and beauty and majesty in the bodies of fat humans, too. Fat bodies dance and master elegant yoga poses. They swim and run and ski down snowy mountains with agility. Our size does not dictate the impressiveness or the grace or value with which we move. Even more, our ability does not dictate our worth. A person whose size is linked to a disability is a good representation of the image of God.

What I want to say to Shedd, and to many other proponents of diet devotionals—and, really, what I want to say to my past self—is this: it's not our bodies that need to change, but our *perception* of our bodies. Eating and living the way God wants us to live means changing how we understand a good body. Rather than trying to make our bodies good, *imago Dei* means that our bodies are already good, and attempting to make them into something else disrespects the handiwork of the Creator.

Shedd's book is not without its moments of truth. He cautions against giving unilateral medical or nutrition advice, acknowledging that all bodies are different and that everyone responds differently. He says, "Every body is different—you won't look like the ideal, you will look like you."[18] Yet he still seems to believe that all bodies will be thin or are meant to be thin. He also poetically points out that the "fat man doesn't love himself—hate begets hate and day by day he sits by the side of the road, alone."[19] For Shedd, ending the hate means ending the fat. I'd rather just end the hate.

Shedd was the first in the modern devotional-diet industry. He was certainly not the last. A stroll through a bookstore or a search online will reveal the countless ways people have come up with to make losing weight a spiritual and moral imperative for the Christian.

Gwen Shamblin wrote *The Weight Down Diet* in 1997, and it swept the nation, spawning church-based weight-loss groups and yielding skyrocketing sales. Although some places, such as Wheaton

College in Illinois, did refuse to support the book, claiming that it could encourage a pattern of disordered eating, it remained popular.[20] In three years, Shamblin sold one million copies. She seems to see herself as a prophet in the wilderness, speaking harsh truths and calling God's people back to purity. She says that her "major concern in life has been to warn the churches against corruption."[21] Shamblin's approach to losing weight God's way does not involve any type of nutritional advice or encouragement to exercise. Rather, Shamblin says we must learn to distinguish our physical hunger from our spiritual hunger and eat only when we are physically hungry. She makes it clear throughout her books that you can eat whatever you want; it is simply important to eat only enough to make you full. Sin as related to food, according to Shamblin, is "telling people that God requires you to exercise, that brownies are evil, that sour cream is evil."[22] If I did not know Shamblin's conclusion that fatness is a sin, I would agree with her here. Shamblin misses the mark, though. She believes people are fat because they do not understand their own body and are feeding spiritual hungers with too much food.

The story of Exodus tells us that God is on the side of the oppressed and desires that they be free from bondage and the oppressive rule of others.

Gwen Shamblin uses the Exodus story to promise deliverance from bondage as well, but in her telling of the story, the bondage is a fat body, and the promised land is thinness. The real bondage here is the fear of and shame about our bodies instilled in us by a society that profits from this fear and shame. When the fear and shame go uncritiqued within the church and the church signs on to promoting a body ideal, then the church becomes complicit and makes a mockery of the liberating message of Jesus by adding religious weight to the cultural message of shame. Shamblin describes her own weight history as being a "thin eater" as a child, gaining the freshman fifteen, and never being more than twenty pounds over her college weight.[23] Yet she speaks as if she has experience with and authority on life in a fat body or understands what it means to lose a significant amount of weight. In this, she is speaking from a place of power. She is afraid to become one of the marginalized (fat) and uses her voice to further oppress.

Shamblin fell out of favor in 2000 after she sent her followers an email in which she denied the Trinity. Her publisher canceled her forthcoming book. In a response about the controversy, Shamblin told *Christianity Today*, "People don't care about this. They don't care about the Trinity. What the women want is weight loss. They care about their bodies being temple [sic] and their lives turned over to the Lord. That's what my ministry is about."[24] Shamblin viewed the size of our bodies as more important than foundational Christian teaching and theology. Her goal was to sell books that promised people, women especially, that they could make their bodies thin. In doing so, she certainly didn't offer a faithful view of the image of God in all of us.

There were, and are still, many other books like this. Weight loss books are a profitable business within both the diet and Christian literature genres. Rick Warren's book *The Daniel Plan* also has been a best seller and won the Evangelical Christian Publishers Association's 2015 Book of the Year award. In addition to the book being inspired by the baptism of fat people, Warren called on Dr. Oz for medical guidance. While Dr. Oz is a physician, he is most known for his talk show, where he promotes products for weight loss. He has said on his show that a variety of foods and products work to achieve weight loss. These claims earned him a seat before a congressional hearing in which he was questioned on the way he talked about weight-loss products on his show. Democratic senator Claire McCaskill of Missouri told him, "The scientific community is almost monolithic against you in terms of the efficacy of the three products that you've called mira-cles."[25] Dr. Oz's response was that he feels his job is to be a cheerleader for people and give them hope that they can achieve their weight-loss goals. But false hope is no friend. There is no proven way for people to lose a significant amount of weight and keep it off. False hope sets up a system in which peo-ple feel defeated.

This is not the hope of God. God's hope says that the Spirit is within us, no matter the size of our body. That there is a purpose and a plan and a reason for our life. There are no conditions that exclude us from being able to hear God's call on our life or respond because of the size of our body. God's hope says you are loved and full of dignity and worth just as you are. You don't need to buy any miracle treat-ment first.

One of my favorite pastimes is to wander thrift stores, looking for treasures. I dig through the books, looking for diet devotionals. My purpose is multifold. One, I don't want to pay for them at a bookstore, but I want to be able to read them as reference materials for my work. Two, I don't want them to be easily available to others who are trying to figure out whether God loves their fat body. And, three, I turn them into craft projects. On days when I am feeling especially overwhelmed by the work I do, when I have had one too many comments from strangers on the internet quoting Proverbs 23 at me and telling me I should put a knife to my throat if I am given to appetite, I turn to art for a bit of creative stress relief. I flip through the thrifted diet devotional books and find a page to transform. I note certain words and circle them and block out all the other words—creating a new message on the page. It is found poetry.

One of my favorite transformations came from the book *Made to Crave* by Lysa TerKeurst. I first picked up TerKeurst's book in the midst of a crisis of faith, trying to find something to anchor me back to a faith with which I was struggling. I couldn't tell from the summary I read on the library's e-book website that it was a weight-loss book. I must have missed the subtitle: "Satisfying Your Deepest Desires with God, Not Food." When I started reading it, I threw my tablet down in frustration. In chapter 2 of her book, TerKeurst talks about her morning weigh-in and how she takes off even her ponytail holder in an attempt to make the scale read as low as possible. She chastises herself for eating a cinnamon roll and admits that she ate more than one, more than was needed to satisfy her hunger. She believes that once she's had one treat, her goal for the day (to become thin) is already wrecked. I took this page and covered up most of the words until it read, "Strip off everything: today I try again. My resolve: love and another day." TerKeurst stripped off her ponytail holder in an attempt to reduce her body's weight; my hope is that I can strip off the weight of shame that comes with messages that say my body must be thin in order for the day to be about love—of God, my neighbors, and even my enemies.

It has been over half a century since Shedd's book was published, but the predominant narrative has not changed much. We tend to use more politically correct language, but we as a society still hate fatness, and there are still Christians writing books devoted to becoming thin or using fatness as an easy example of what it looks like to lack self-control.

For so many years of my life, I woke up and went to bed praying about my body. I prayed for strength of conviction and sometimes prayed to care enough to be convicted. I confessed sin and lamented the way I failed to reduce my body into something smaller and more God-honoring. I felt guilt for hating gym class and guilt for enjoying the popcorn shrimp they served in the school lunch line on Fridays. I felt the most guilt that for all my devotion and desire to serve God, I was still an embarrassment to God and the church because my body would not adjust. It would not conform to the ideal.

These days, my relationship with my body is gentler. My prayers are filled with other requests: healing for children whose lives know pain, comfort for people who feel discouraged, and the ability for me to see where God is moving and to join that work. I have so much more space—in my head, in my day—to focus on God's work in this world when my first prayer isn't always about my body. I can praise God for the way I am uniquely equipped and gifted to serve my community in the body I have.

One day, I hope my thrift-store hunts turn up more books about living well in the body we have than books about trying to make our body different.

NOTES

1. Carole Lewis with W. Terry Whalin, *First Place* (Ventura, CA: Regal, 2001), front matter.

2. Carole Lewis with Marcus Brotherton, *First Place 4 Health: Discover a New Way to Healthy Living* (Ventura, CA: Regal, 2008), 15.

3. Lynne Gerber, *Seeking the Straight and Narrow* (Chicago: University of Chicago Press, 2011), Kindle edition, location 2227.

4. Lewis and Whalin, *First Place*, 83.

5. Heather Bauer and Kathy Matthews, *Bread Is the Devil: Win the Weight Loss Battle by Taking Control of Your Diet Demons* (New York: St. Martin's, 2012).

6. Bauer and Matthews, *Bread Is the Devil*, inside jacket.

7. Bauer and Matthews, *Bread Is the Devil*, inside jacket.

8. Bauer and Matthews, *Bread Is the Devil*, 1.

9. Balcony Publishing, "About the Author: Dr. Charlie Shedd," https://tinyurl.com/yan44cms.

10. Charlie W. Shedd, *Pray Your Weight Away* (Philadelphia: J. B. Lippincott, 1957).

11. Shedd, *Pray Your Weight Away*, back jacket.

12. Shedd, *Pray Your Weight Away*, back jacket.

13. Shedd, *Pray Your Weight Away*.

14. Shedd, *Pray Your Weight Away*, 15–16.

15. Shedd, *Pray Your Weight Away*, 9–10.

16. William Randolph Mueller, "Of Obesity and Election," *Christian Century* 75 (1958): 1366–68.

17. Shedd, *Pray Your Weight Away*, 44.

18. Shedd, *Pray Your Weight Away*, 50.

19. Shedd, *Pray Your Weight Away*, 48.

20. Lauren F. Winner, "The Weigh and the Truth," *Christianity Today*, September 4, 2000, p. 54.

21. Beverley James, "Love God, Lose Weight," *Toronto Star*, November 11, 2000.

22. Winner, "The Weigh and the Truth," 51.

23. Winner, "The Weigh and the Truth," 51.

24. Todd Kennedy and John W. Starnes, "Gwen Shamblin in the Balance," *Christianity Today*, October 23, 2000, 15.

25. "Weight-Loss Product Advertising," C-SPAN.org, June 17 2014, https://tinyurl.com/y9thmmv5.

8

FAT GIRLS AND RIGHTEOUS FOXES

Content note: This chapter includes descriptions of sexual assault, rape, and spiritual and emotional abuse.

I sat on a log near the lake where my youth group was spending the week for our summer camp. Next to me were seven or so other teenagers. The topic of our study that afternoon was preparing ourselves for a godly marriage. The adult male leader looked at us and got very serious: "I'm going to tell you something, girls. Guys need your help." I was fully invested in doing everything I could to become a godly wife for a future husband, so I leaned in close. "Our eyes will be drawn to your bodies. If you put effort into making your face look its best, that will help us keep our thoughts pure." I leaned back, disappointed. This didn't apply to me. I was fat; men didn't look at my body anyway. I hardly ever wore makeup as a teenager or young adult. My mom didn't really wear it, and aside from a few Mary Kay parties, I had never really learned how to apply it. Plus, I figured it didn't matter much. No amount of mascara or foundation would hide the fact that I was fat, and I assumed that is what really mattered. In another church class for teenage girls only, we read *Lady in Waiting: Becoming God's Best While Waiting for Mr. Right* (by Jackie Kendall and Debbie Jones), which talks about inner beauty. Yet everything around me said that outer beauty still mattered a whole lot, even in the church. The man telling me at summer church camp to think carefully about the appearance of my body and face only confirmed this narrative.

Years later, the summer after my sophomore year in college, I listened to my pastor preach a series on dating, love, marriage, and sex. I was single at the time and always had been, but I hoped that maybe there was something there for me to learn. The pastor explained that men are hardwired for sex and cannot stop once they start. "Girls," he told us, "we need you to stop it before it starts." The pastor talked about the way we dress, the way we talk and move. He asked us to insist on not being alone with a date and to understand if a guy canceled a date on us; perhaps the guy had found enough self-control to know he couldn't handle being in our presence that night without having sex. I was listening but was convinced this was another lesson I did not need to learn. I was fat; men did not want to have sex with me. At nineteen, my body had never been a temptation to anyone. I had to come believe that if I were to ever get married, I would be able to bypass many of these problems with men's lust.

When I was eighteen, I received a compliment from a stranger at a grocery store. He told me I had nice hair. My initial instinct was to assume he was being sarcastic. I combed my fingers through my hair, checking for knots or stray hairs or the name tag from the Bible study I'd just left tangled up in my long hair. "Is there something wrong with it?" I asked. He repeated his simple compliment: "No, it's nice." This back-and-forth happened a couple of times before I realized he was being serious; I offered a simple thank you and walked away. A few months ago, I ran across copies of my high school senior pictures. My hair is long and smooth and shiny. It is nice—beautiful even. I didn't know that then.

At twenty, I wrote in my journal "that maybe one

day I'd find a guy who married me for my personality and the rest would be some obligation or something." I had been taught that godly men would see my love for God and find that beautiful, my inner beauty. At the same time, I believed non-Christian men only cared about physical beauty and having sex. I assumed this meant that my fat body—which no one ever suggested was desirable—was safe from those who only wanted sex and that godly men would be able to see my character and not be dismayed by the drape of my stomach. As I listened to my pastor warn it was the woman's job to stop any premarital sex from happening, I thought about how nice it was that I did not have to fight off the wrong kind of men.

The Bible is full of women whose beauty is a part of their story. Abraham lies about Sarah because of her beauty. Rahab and Esther use their beauty as a tool to bring freedom and rescue. Rebecca's beauty earns her a proposal almost instantly. Then there are the sisters, Rachel and Leah. Rachel's beauty is praised in contrast to the homely Leah. The story in Genesis tells us that "Rachel was beautiful in form and appearance" (Genesis 29:17, ESV). Jacob loves Rachel and proposes on the spot. She's got the whole package, and it lands her a proposal from the newest bachelor in town. Rachel did not get the lesson on summer camp to focus on her face. Her body, her form, is noticed, as well as her appearance. I find a bit of a kindred spirit in Leah, whose lack of beauty means she is less valued—as a person, as a potential wife—than her more beautiful sister, Rachel. Leah was certainly part of the group of people who greeted Jacob. Yet, she is unnoticed by Jacob or at least dismissed next to her lovelier sister. I doubt she is surprised. She has lived her life being the older sister and the second best. She has seen the pattern when it comes to relationships: outward beauty often wins. Yet in her culture, there is no option to develop a full and meaningful single life. Singleness is poverty. She needs to marry. Her father, Laban, has a plan. Laban switches Leah into Rachel's place on the wedding night, and now Jacob has more brides than he bargained for, eventually getting Rachel after another week.

I wonder what that first night and then the following week must have been like for Leah. I wonder which hurt more: the first night, when Jacob acted out a desire she knew was not for her, or all the days that followed, in which she was reminded over and over again that she was not the prize. Her financial future had been secured, but the loneliness and desires of the heart must have lived on and surely have been amplified. More times than I can count, I have been the person who is overlooked or ignored when a group conversation turns to matchmaking or potential love interests. Not to be considered an option is painful. To be used by others is all the more gut-wrenching. It is confirmation that your heart doesn't matter because your body failed to win the genetics jackpot.

As the years pass, it becomes clear that while Rachel has the beauty, Leah has the fertility. She births children one after another. They do not earn her the love of Jacob. That is still the longing of her heart, reflected in her names for her sons: Reuben, "for now my husband will love me" (Genesis 29:32), and Levi in the hopes that this time her husband will attach to her (29:34). Judah is her fourth child, and she says, "This time I will praise the Lord." For a brief moment, it seems that perhaps Leah can be content. Maybe four sons has earned her some of the tenderness from Jacob she so deeply desires, maybe she has truly reached a point where she is okay without it, or maybe she is so busy with four young boys that the desires of her own heart get pushed to the side.

Then the competition starts again. Rachel, unable to have children and jealous of her sister's womb, sends her servant Bilhah to Jacob. Leah responds by sending her servant Zilpah. This is rape. Zilpah and

Bilhah are forced to endure Jacob's sexual advances whether they want to or not. Four traumatized women, four more sons for Jacob—there is no romance in this story. It is a fight about women's bodies and how they look and what they can do and who is better because of those traits. Zilpah and Bilhah get trampled as Rachel and Leah try to prove who is better. When all the births are done, Jacob has at least one daughter and twelve sons—the twelve tribes of Israel. Judah, the son who will take a place in the lineage of Jesus, is the son of Jacob and Leah. Leah, despite her lack of beauty and her complicity in this tragic story, stands in the lineage of Jesus.

In the story of the patriarchs, roles get frequently reversed. The second son is often the one with the blessing, even though cultural norms say blessing belongs to the firstborn son. Isaac, not Ishmael. Jacob, not Esau. Here, the first daughter gets the ultimate blessing, not the one whose beauty made her stand out. Leah did not do anything to earn this blessing. She is as complicit in the oppression of Zilpah and Bilhah as Rachel and Jacob are. She and the rest of the matriarchs are as human and flawed and broken and relatable as the patriarchs. There is no nobility in being unattractive. There is no formula that makes unattractive people better humans.

If anything, Leah should have had more compassion for the others, knowing too well the gut-wrenching pain of her body being used when no desire was behind it. Nevertheless, she stands in the lineage of Jesus. Beauty is praised throughout Scripture, but it is not what defines our worth or our place in this world or our ability to be a part of God's plan.

No one at church ever told me outright that I needed to be beautiful in order to get married. The goal presented to me as a teenager was to be gentle and quiet, and that would be beautiful. The verse often quoted to us was 1 Peter 3:4: "the unfading beauty of a gentle and quiet spirit" (NIV). If we were gentle and quiet, men would see our unfading beauty. The beginning of 1 Peter 3 even says that this gentleness has the power to convert men to Christ. Nothing about my body ever felt gentle. The sheer force of gravity when my body enters spaces causes floors to creak and chairs to groan; quiet does not seem in the realm of possibility. Halfway through my senior year of high school, I wrote in my journal, "I talk about wanting to get married, but somehow I doubt I ever will. No guy deserves to have a girl who is as fat as I am. The guy deserves someone he can hold close." I often felt very matter-of-fact about things like this—accepting them as simple truths and finding no reason to get sad about it. I just needed to accept my reality and learn to live with the limited possibilities that my body presented me in terms of future relationships.

When I read that now, I want so badly to be able to tell the younger me the truth: You are a woman whose strength and beauty and power cannot be measured by something as basic as a scale. You are worth far more than the sum of the pounds that make up your body. Gentleness isn't daintiness. Quietness is not smallness. Even more, being gentle and quiet is not all the Bible asks of people of God, even women of God.

Knowing that truth has radically changed who I am and how I interact with the world. I wonder who I would have been if I had known earlier that I am capable and strong and full of the power that comes with embracing God's abundant grace and love.

DATING WHILE FAT

In fifth grade, while I was sitting at lunch with my classmates, two boys were sitting across from me and laughing quietly with each other while glancing in my direction. Finally, one of them spoke up: "You're the first girl in our class to have boobs!" he howled with excitement. I blushed furiously and turned my head down to eat the rest of my lunch in as much solitude as a school cafeteria can offer. My fat body grew breasts early. A picture of me around the same age, playing in the pool with a friend, shows the inadequacies of my childhood swimsuit. It appears alarmingly low-cut. I was unaware of the way it looked until years later, when a family friend shared pictures of the day with my mother.

The shame of fatness and the shame that comes with having a female body are inextricably linked, one identity adding nuances to the others. Much of the fat-shame women experience is rooted in how sexually appealing, or not, men find that body. My fifth-grade classmate sexualized my adolescent body, and as an adult, anti-fatness can often show up in fetishized notions of the fat female body or viewing fat females as asexual. My fatness is an ever-present part of my dating life, no matter how much self-confidence I maintain.

I had my first date when I was twenty, which in hindsight seems incredibly young. But being single for all of middle and high school and early college felt like an eternity. One thing felt oppressively true: I was too fat to be attractive, too fat to be quiet and gentle, too fat to love. Since that first date at twenty, I have had one long-term relationship, one short one, and a small handful of other dates. I have ventured into the world of online dating—Craigslist before we got scared off by the serial killers, OkCupid, eHarmony, Match, others. I met a few guys from dating sites who were great but weren't a great match. I read the profiles of countless men I wasn't interested in and a few I was. For most men, fatness is a deal breaker. Actually, I should say that fatness seems to be a deal breaker for most Christian men. I used to believe that non-Christian men did not care anything about a woman's character and just wanted a super model, and that Christian men would put aside beauty ideals in favor of a Christian woman. In my experience, the reverse has almost always been true. If I were to draw a Venn diagram from my experience, the circle for Men Who Love Jesus and the circle for Men Who Would Consider Dating Fat Women barely touch.

Of all the topics I write about, the way Christian men view fat women is perhaps the one that women want to talk about the most. I've heard story after story of women who have been told, as I have, by Christian men that they aren't interested in dating women with obvious sin in her life. By sin, they mean fatness, which they assume to be the result of lack of self-control or lack of care for her temple. These men couch their anti-fat bias in Christianese and walk away feeling holy and as if they'd led a woman a step closer to the narrow path toward heaven. Women bear the worst of society's demands for what we must look like in order to be acceptable. This sort of oppression transfers into the church without much pushback from the altar or the Sunday school room. I am sure that men deal with fat bias as well. I have heard from a few who have said as much. I have seen men face more and more body shame and stigma in recent years, which is not the type of equality I desire. I am even less familiar with what fat bias looks like outside of heterosexual, cisgender relationships, but I am confident that fat bias creeps in even there. (I am speaking of only heterosexual relationships between cis-gender people here, because it was the only scenario that was considered a possibility in my youth.) Fat is seen as a socially acceptable reason to reject a person as a romantic partner, regardless of gender or type of relationship.

My experience is obviously just mine. I know many people, Christian and not, who have met and loved and married in bodies of various size. My reality—single and in my mid-thirties—is not universal to all fat Christian women. Reclaiming my body as made in the image of God is vital to my ability to reject relationships that don't value my full humanity.

As a teenager, I was very involved in church. I went on mission trips and showed up for Sunday school and for Sunday-night and Wednesday-evening activities. I was on the youth leadership team and led committees. I went on ski retreats, summer retreats, and one-day retreats. I sat in the audience at camps near sandy lakes in Florida and at events in the mountains of Tennessee. I sat with fellow youth missionaries in various places across the country. Over and over again, I heard the speaker or pastor proclaim from the stage that he had a "righteous fox" for a wife. It was as if they had sent out a memo to all male youth leaders that they must describe their wives in that way. I participated in classes for teenage girls at our church where we were taught, specifically and explicitly, that godly women would be inwardly beautiful, but there was little to no discussion on how that differs from outward beauty.

I believe that these pastors and teachers had good intentions. Men and teenage boys were taught that women want to be and feel beautiful, so they praised beauty where they saw it. The church told men to look for someone who loves God, and she would be beautiful to them. So when they found a beautiful Christian woman, her love of God and her outward beauty seemed meant to be.

All I heard, though, as I sat and listened to the pastors praise their beautiful wives was that in order for me to marry a man of God (and if I was lucky, one who would be a pastor, because really, that was the goal of almost every '90s girl in youth group), I had to be both righteous *and* a fox. The wives of youth-camp speakers were typically present at the conferences, or the speaker included a picture of his wife in his PowerPoint presentation.

I looked: none of them were fat.

Whatever the men believed about their ability to see godliness and inner beauty, the wives all looked too similar. Something else was going on. Righteousness was not enough.

But I held out hope. Maybe I didn't need to marry a pastor—just an ordinary guy who loved God. Maybe righteousness would be enough for him. Maybe someone would find my inner beauty good enough to put up with my fat body, to see beyond it, to love me in spite of it. I had no frame of reference at the time for a man who would one day look at me and delight in the roundness of my thighs.

My involvement in any kind of romantic relationship during middle school and high school can be quickly summed up: in middle school, someone once told me that a boy liked me, and I assumed he meant it mockingly. And that's it. If there was any other interest from anyone, I never heard about it. I wasn't really looking, to be honest. At church, I got a steady diet of *True Love Waits* and purity culture that taught me that if I waited and had enough faith, God would send me someone who saw my inner beauty—something I believed into my college years, despite the fact that I had yet to see any real evidence that fat girls got married, too.

I was convinced that a godly man would see through my fat to who I really was.

Beginning with the fall of my freshman year of college and going through the spring of my junior year, I experienced a time in my faith that I can only describe as *sweet*. To this day, those years are unmatched in terms of the easy peace with which I lived my faith. I very literally fell asleep and woke up praying. I read Scripture morning, noon, and night. I was checking no list; I had just been captivated by the person of Jesus Christ.

A couple of years into this season of my life, I met someone. He almost immediately declared his interest in me. We spent hours talking and getting to know each other. I prayed about it, and as I was taught to do, I asked for my father's advice. He gave his blessing. Daniel (not his real name) and I officially became a couple a few months after meeting. He told me he was in love with me. I was ecstatic. We'd originally met online. We talked first online and then on the phone. He drove the few hours between us to visit a few months later, and we made the relationship official.

About nine months into the relationship, I wrote in my journal that he had told me he wanted to have sex with me but knew it needed to wait until marriage, something important to me at the time. He, unlike me, was not a virgin. Nevertheless, I was shocked by his admission of attraction, even after months of dating. I still firmly believed that he had found something desirable about only my personality and that any physical temptations would be nonexistent because of my fatness. It was shortly after we began dating that I stumbled into the online fat fashion community, trying to find a way to appear more attractive for my new boyfriend.

One fall day, I had a couple of days off work, and Daniel came to visit. We sat on the couch for a while and talked before he stood up, took my hand, and led me to my room. I expressed doubt at the wisdom of lying on a bed together, my pastor's words from a couple of years before ringing in my ears, but he assured me we would just cuddle. It happened slowly and gently, but my quiet requests for him to wait were met with his gentle, soft reassurances that everything was fine, that I was fine. It took me years to look back on that moment and call it *rape*, rather than blame myself for not saying no effectively.

When I read years later that true consent is enthusiastic and ongoing, I knew I hadn't actually consented to sex with Daniel. At the time, I felt a deep sense of shame. My desire had been not to have sex until I married, and I felt I had failed to try hard enough to stop him. I had failed at keeping our relationship pure, failed at keeping myself pure, failed at keeping him pure.

He called me later, worried that he had gone too far, worried that I was not okay. I dismissed his fears and assured him that he'd done nothing wrong, trying to protect at least one of us from the shame and guilt. I tried to fix the shame and convince myself that it had all been consensual by embracing the sexual side of our relationship in the years that followed. I told myself I was a willing and eager participant. I told myself that my desires not to have sex until marriage didn't really matter and weren't that important, since I would marry him anyway. Eventually sex became the way I held on to him—convinced that if he wanted me even when I was fat, that he must really want me, that this was going to work.

Those years were filled with doubts and troubles and red flags I might have been better able to see if I'd not been convinced that the first man who said he loved me had to be the one who was godly enough to see my beauty. I couldn't imagine a world in which a man would desire my body if he did not truly love me.

I was convinced I was going to marry him, and the intoxication of having someone who seemingly saw my righteousness and found my body beautiful—foxy, if you will—was strong. I remember standing over my bathroom sink, burning journal pages where I had finally decided to write out the things that worried me about the relationship: he did not seem completely honest; I had yet to meet his family or any of his close friends; dates were frequently canceled; there was a room in his house I was not allowed to enter; he flirted frequently with my friends. I shoved the pain of those things down every time. I looked at his hand holding mine and told myself I was overreacting. I told myself that he had to be the one, and I just needed to be patient while God worked everything together for good. He rarely needed to apologize for any of his bad behavior; I hardly ever called him out on it. I would not admit it then, but this relationship was toxic. It was emotionally abusive. I failed to acknowledge this fact despite a mountain of evidence. I believed that I was honoring God by staying in the relationship with the first man who had convinced me through his physical desires he was so godly he could see my beauty.

The danger of purity culture for fat girls in particular is that it implies that only godly men could want a fat woman, that only godly men can see inner beauty in the body of a fat woman. I believed that I was so unattractive that I was safe both from being asked out by non-Christian men who only wanted sex and, even more, from violent attacks. I believed I was too ugly even to rape. As a result, I was prepared to accept and embrace the attention of any man who saw my vulnerability and trust. That trust was violated.

My relationship with Daniel lasted about four years, and then it ended when I found him with another woman and could no longer rationalize away the warning signs. He had cheated, repeatedly. We continued to talk on and off for years in a long, drawn-out good-bye with a thousand missteps as I fought to regain a sense of myself and break my addiction to him. The end of that relationship and the realization that I had never been loved completely by him, despite my trust in God and fervent belief that this was the path God had ordained for my life, ushered in a crisis of faith that shook me to my core. Eventually I came out on the other side with a stronger, if radically different, faith.

Despite the pain, I learned from the relationship with Daniel that my body could be desired. I left that experience knowing that my body is beautiful—that my body is not asexual or reserved for fetishes. God brings beauty from ashes, strength from pain, and gladness from mourning—for our lives and our bodies, too.

BIBLICAL BEAUTY

In the Song of Songs, there are verses that describe the beauty of the woman—verses whose metaphors defy prescription into any generation's beauty ideals. Early on, the lover compares the woman with a horse (Song 1:9). In chapter 4, he compares her to nature—plants, animals, fruits. None of these match the image of a contemporary model or even the girl-next-door image of beauty. Then the guy in this song of love says:

> Your rounded thighs are like jewels,
> the work of a master hand.
> . . . .
> Your belly is a heap of wheat,
> . . . .
> How beautiful and pleasant you are,
> O Loved one, with all your delights!
> (Song of Songs 7:1, 2, 6, ESV)

One of my favorite things about the physical descriptions of the bodies of the two lovers in Song of Songs is that you have absolutely no idea what either person looks like. Breasts like fawns, a head like a camel, and a nose that's a tower are not exactly twenty-first-century beauty metaphors. Yes, there are plenty of descriptions of the bodies of both the men and the women that lead the reader to imagine someone slender, but there are also round thighs and bellies that are heaps. It is also important to note that the woman describes herself as dark and beautiful. Regardless of size or skin tone or any other factor: beauty is attainable, and it looks nothing like the magazines.

My favorite thing to do with our concept of beauty is to dissect it, to analyze all the ways it is problematic and how the praise and pursuit of it has so often caused pain through the millennia. But sometimes I stop and force myself to see beauty the way God sees it, the way the lover of Song of Songs sees it. I close my eyes and imagine what it must mean to positively compare a loved one's beauty to a camel and a tower. I ponder what endearing characteristic is found in those metaphors. Perhaps the lover would call my body a whale, powerful and graceful when given the right environment in which to thrive. Heaping bellies and rounded thighs are things I possess. That's what my body looks like. My body—my beauty—is reflected in the pages of the Bible's most sensual book.

Beauty often still feels inaccessible to me, but since I read Song of Songs with this fresh vision a few years ago, I am beginning to see the beauty of my own body a bit more clearly. The multiple ways the loved one is described in this book prove that there is no singular standard for beauty. Seeing my own beauty will not change the way my body exists in this world, with its own strict rules about what is acceptable, but seeing the way the lover delights reminds me that it is possible to have that fullness in a relationship. In this book of passionate love, there is a place for all bodies. Our shapes, our sizes, and our skin tones are all celebrated in this one beautiful, inspired work of literature.

I don't know if I will ever be in a relationship again; I would like to be. If such a time comes, I will fully expect that the man I am with takes joy and pleasure in my body in a way that celebrates the uniqueness of my body and the delights it can give.

Looking back, I can see now how the Christian teaching I heard set me up for a toxic relationship by failing to define beauty and righteousness in healthy ways. I believed that the pattern was (1) love God; (2) man will find you desirable; (3) live happily ever after. All that I had been taught about waiting, about purity, about righteousness told me that if I truly loved God, I would be seen by someone else who truly loved God. All that the world told me about beauty led me to believe that no man without God would be able to see past the flaw of my fat body to my soul. I was convinced I had no reason to worry about ending up in a bad relationship. Only a man truly in tune to God would fall in love with my fat body. Only a man of strong faith would ever even desire to be with me.

So when I met Daniel, it only took a few months of infatuated bliss for me to shrug off the warning signs. He desired my body, so I assumed he must have godly vision.

That relationship changed my life. It wounded me in real ways, but it also opened my eyes to the ways I had misunderstood the relationship between fatness, beauty, godliness, and desire. It was the end of this relationship that drove me to an altar for a tear-filled prayer. You remember the story I told in the introduction: the one that ended with a woman coming to pray with me and asking God to help me release the sin of my fatness.

We have to start teaching our children and youth that people are attracted to different things. Do a study on Song of Songs with the young people in your life, endure the giggles, and point out all the ways that the lover describes beauty. Deconstruct the world's idea of beauty. Don't talk about inner beauty in that conversation; just point out that outward beauty isn't a one-size-fits-all dress. (You can find a few more suggestions for how to talk to children and youth about fatness in the resources section at the end of this book.) Fat people deserve to know that they can be beautiful, too—both because it will empower them and because if we don't, we risk making them more susceptible to abuse. People deserve to know that their attraction to fat people is not a fetish and is not shameful. I've received a handful of notes from men who read my work on Christian fat acceptance and finally find some freedom in knowing there is nothing wrong with them for finding fat women attractive. The church needs more men to stand up and speak to other men about the ways we objectify women and assume a universal standard of beauty.

BEAUTY AND CULTURE

My eyes have always been the body part that receives the most compliments. Men I have dated stare into them in somewhat of a trance and announce their beauty as if they are the first to see this and would like to share their great discovery. I like my eyes, too. So when I started experimenting with makeup in college, eye shadow and mascara came first. I would not leave the house until my lashes were dark and full. I read online makeup tutorials to learn which eye shadow colors would bring out the deep blue of my eyes. I wanted the perfect mascara that would frame my eyes and draw all the attention there—away from my arms and stomach.

I stuck with my eye makeup routine for years until my eyes got too dry and my bank account too empty to be able to justify the money spent on contacts, and I switched back to glasses. There did not seem to be as much of a point with eye makeup after that. I bought dark-rimmed glasses with a small cat eyes, and I turned my makeup attention to my lips. I went with subtle shades first, and before I knew it, I was buying deep reds, dark purples, and bright pinks. My eye makeup routine had always been about highlighting what I considered my best feature. This was different. This felt bold. I marveled at the way I felt more confident, now that I was walking around with highlighted lips—my mouth, what I use to eat. And not only that, but I left my mark behind. Bright, bold colors showed up on coffee cups, napkins, and the tips of straws. I was no longer just highlighting a feature on my body that met culturally acceptable definitions of beauty; I was doing something that made me stand out. It felt brave and a bit loud, even if it was just lipstick.

As a teen, I tried desperately to be gentle and quiet in the hopes I would truly be seen for who I was on the inside. These days, I wear homemade shirts that say "Fat Feminist," and I apply bold lipstick. I talk more but am still pretty quiet. I take selfies and post them on Instagram, showing off my outfit or the new lipstick or the earrings I picked up at the thrift store. I grew up believing that no one would want to look at me. I have found freedom and confidence in putting my own image out into the world. People can look, but it is not for them. It is my way to reclaim beauty and wrestle with all of its problematic ties while still acknowledging that I am allowed to claim it.

When I was a kid, my teachers and pastors tried to instill in me the importance of character, but in the process, they didn't help me find ways to love and honor my body, and that had some damaging effects. My hope is that we will learn better ways to teach our children about what to expect from relationships, and treat them as whole, embodied people. Our character matters, but our lived experience in our bodies of various sizes and skin tones and identities and abilities affects the way we navigate this world. I want us to work to make sure that all people know their bodies are valuable and loved and even beautiful in the eyes of the God who created all things.

9

THE CHURCH THAT EATS TOGETHER STAYS TOGETHER

In seminary, I spent an academic year living in accidental, intentional community with my roommates and a few of our apartment-complex neighbors. Early in the year, my apartment mates and I invited everyone we saw in the neighborhood to dinner one Sunday night, and within a few weeks, there was a crowd of five to ten people who showed up every Sunday night, straining the limits of our seating and leaving behind a sink full of coffee mugs and teacups at the end of the night. We came from Illinois, Minnesota, Florida, New York, Ghana, and Nigeria. We took turns cooking each week, and whoever didn't cook was responsible for the cleanup. By January, our meals together were frequent. If someone felt like making dinner some night of the week, they'd add a little extra of whatever they were having and invite everyone else along. Sometimes we'd splurge and head out for Mediterranean food at our favorite local restaurant, where the service was slow and the food was delicious. We'd stop on our way to pick up a bottle of wine or two to get us through the long wait for our falafel and dolmas.

Early in the academic year, we shared with each other a bit of our stories. Almost everyone had a story of a struggle with food and bodies. Without any formal decision or discussion on the matter, we ate together without shame that year. We feasted on multicourse meals at holidays. We rummaged through cabinets and fridges to pull together a hearty soup in the midst of blizzards and storms. We had simple suppers of bread, cheese, and fruit during the hot summer months, opening the windows on either side of the non-air-conditioned apartment to let the breeze flow through. We never talked about what the homemade cheesecake would do to our hips. We didn't voice concerns that seconds were wrong. When we heard that another community about twenty minutes away that typically had weekly dinners together was struggling, we packed up bags of groceries and took our meal on the road—offering the community and welcome to them in the form of the healing, life-giving power of feasting together.

It was beautiful to dine together in such freedom that year. I don't know how or why we settled into such an easy and life-giving rhythm of dining together. It was a gift of grace. We were all single students who had hours on end to sit in relative quiet while we read textbooks and wrote papers and waited for the soup to simmer. We were all pursuing advanced degrees focused on helping people. We all cared deeply about solving some of the hurts of the world. Perhaps that tuned us in to the wounds we saw in each other and made us aware of the ways we could walk gently around and offer nourishing community. The year was truly a gift. That context is unlikely to be repeated in my life, but showing up in spaces together, sharing a table, and being intentional to see the wounds of others (and show my own) so that we can nourish and care for each other are disciplines I can implement, no matter my context.

The community I enjoyed that year was unique in a variety of ways, but the ability to eat together without the oh-too-common trappings of body shame dominating the meal was a true blessing.

FEASTING TOGETHER

Certainly the Bible is full of stories of *just enough* food: manna for one day, sometimes two, but never three; the oil and flour that are just enough for the next loaf of bread to feed Elijah and the widow and her son. Yet there is also feasting. In the very beginning, all of the food of the garden of Eden but the one tree was given to Adam and Eve for food. There was only one restriction, and it did not prevent abundance. As the story of the people of God continues, we see that they feast for various reasons. They feast to celebrate. They feast to remember. They feast to worship God. There is a place for abundant food even within a community that has frequently known want, perhaps especially in that community. There is a place for abundant food in the story of a people that includes King Eglon and the people of Sodom, who abused their abundance. Abundance and feasting are a necessary part of the way we gather together as a community, especially as a community of faith, and it has been that way since the very beginning.

In our contemporary churches, feasting is a well-known part of how we do life together. When I was growing up, my church did dinner together every Wednesday night. My family didn't often attend, but on the weeks I was there, I noticed that there was always a large collection of to-go boxes headed out the back door. The church made sure that even those who were homebound and unable to join the common table got to share in the meal. Preparing a potluck dish is one of my favorite things. It is a way I get to know a community and share with them a bit of who I am. I enjoy the process of trying to find a recipe that will meet the general taste preferences and dietary restrictions of those with whom I will eat. Sometimes that means a dish with uncommon ingredients. Once, for my first potluck at a new church that was fairly traditional and southern, I brought a large bowl of tabbouleh—a Mediterranean salad of cucumbers and tomatoes and parsley. It almost all came home with me. It was a bit too much for the rest of the congregation to enjoy. Next time, I tried a simpler salad, but I chopped it up and mixed it together and strongly suggested a certain dressing to complement the taste. I managed to win them over with that one, and my salad was requested at every potluck going forward. Feasting together is about listening to each other, getting to know each other, trying out new things, and accepting the offerings that others bring to the table. This is a picture of church; this is a picture of community.

God ordains feast days. Jesus feasts to the point of being accused of gluttony. In Acts, the believers gather and break bread over and over. Yet we can't attend a church dinner without someone joking about the comfort of their waistband (or worse, pointing at ours). Breaking bread together is a foundational part of what Christians do; to exclude people from this practice through body shame is devastating to the body of Christ. We are always in a body. Most people I talk to are hyper-aware of how their body fills the space around them. And they notice, even if they don't want to admit, how others' bodies fill the spaces as well. As we eat, multiple times a day if we are so blessed, we participate in an act that grounds us in the reality of our embodiment. On the joyous days, that act of eating is also a delight to the senses, a way that we may taste and see that the Lord is good. God wants us to enjoy that without shame. God wants us to enjoy each other without worrying that someone else judges our plate or being so preoccupied that we can't enjoy the food in front of us. The people of God, in the Old Testament and New, gather together to eat in a practice that builds unity; body shame disrupts this gift.

I love that Jesus's first miracle is one of excess. He shows up at a wedding and turns the water into wine—the good, strong wine. He says, "We are not done partying yet. We will celebrate some more." Jesus is not afraid of excess, of being accused of gluttony, of dining with people the religious leaders exclude. If this is true, I can imagine that Jesus is not ashamed to be seen with me, a woman whom many say has a body of excess.

Jesus starts his public ministry with a celebration of excess, and the theme shows up again as he teaches his followers. In the parable of the prodigal son in Luke 15:11–32, the younger son wastes his resources on indulgent living. At his lowest moment, he finds himself desiring the same food that the pigs are eating. The son remembers that his father's servants are welcome at the table. He no longer views himself as one worthy to be called a son, but nonetheless expects he can return and be met with food and care. His father has lived a life of an open table. No one is excluded, not even those who waste their inheritance on gluttonous living. When the son returns, he is met with an overjoyed father and a feast. The father does not sit his son down and lecture him on how to live a prudent, moderate life going forward. There are no rules to avoid indulgence as payment for his life of excessive consumption. He is met with a feast. He is called son, seated at a table, and given more than enough. Certainly they did not have an elaborate feast every day. Feasts are for a specified time or reasons, for a celebration. That day, though, there must have been more wine brought out as the party wore on, the celebration far from over.

There is, of course, the other brother—the one who has lived a devoted and moderate life. He, too, has access to the feast. He, too, has access to all his father has. That is not enough for him, however; he demands that those who have not followed the rules not be allowed to feast. That is not how Jesus works. That is not how the father in the parable works. The father reminds his oldest son of the reasons to celebrate and rejoices in the son who has returned. They celebrate with extravagant and abundant food.

When I first began speaking more openly about fat acceptance, I had a friend become angry with me. She accused me of dismissing all of the work she had done to achieve a slimmer body. She said, explicitly, that all of her effort was worth nothing if all we had to do was just accept our bodies. Her fear, I imagine, was that her work had been meaningless. Her striving had been for nothing. Her faithful devotion to a cause had not been needed, and that devotion had been hard and required sacrifice. These are real, valid feelings. When you realize that you have been fighting a battle you didn't need to fight, the temptation can be to keep fighting to save face. Do not let the fear that you missed something stop you from joining the celebration feast that comes with freedom. We are invited to live into the truth of how God sees us—as loved children worthy of a place at the table, no matter what. The older son's life of dedication and quiet, faithful service to his father was not wasted; the father was always there to be with him. He invites him to the celebratory feast of freedom as well.

In the Gospel of Matthew, another biblical story tells of a person turned away from the (metaphorical) table. In Matthew 15, Jesus encounters a Canaanite woman. She comes to Jesus and asks him to heal her daughter who is possessed by demons. The disciples, believing she is less than they because of her Canaanite identity, have no compassion and urge Jesus to send her away. Some theologians and scholars make the argument that Matthew's telling of this story—as a Jew writing to Jews—betrays his preference for Jewish people over the Canaanites. At first, the way the story is told shows Jesus similarly dismissing her: "I was only sent to the children of Israel" is Jesus's first response. She pleads again, "Lord, help me!" Jesus's response seems only crueler: "It is not right to take the children's bread and toss it to the dogs." The woman responds with a strong and defiant response of her own, reminding Jesus that even dogs eat the crumbs that fall from tables. Leticia A. Guardiola-Sáenz, a professor of Christian Scriptures, argues that what the woman in Matthew 15 is saying is that if there is enough food for dogs to eat crumbs, there is also enough for other humans, for her.[1] Some theologians argue that the Canaanite woman corrected Jesus, that she called out his racism and asserted her own humanity. When we believe we are human, we insist on our right to be treated as such, our right to join our community. This encounter empowers the woman to name her own humanity and is instructive to the (Jewish) men present. Jesus affirms her brave assertion of her worth and changes his response to her: "Woman, you have great faith! Your request is granted." He models for the disciples what it means to see the humanity of a person they consider less than themselves.

At some point, the Canaanite woman had to believe a different truth about her body and her worth than the message she heard from others. She asserted her right to join the table, join the community. Our interactions with our own bodies cannot be completely separated from the cultural messages we receive about our bodies. The cultural messages about our bodies cannot be separated from issues of oppression such as racism, colonialism, sexism, and classism. Bodies of all colors, ethnicities, genders, sexual orientations, and abilities are made in the image of God. Any theology or philosophy that fails to welcome all to the table and to name the inherent dignity and worth of each person in our diverse world is flawed at its root.

One of the foundational characteristics of the brand-new church in Acts is that they eat together. We see it first in Acts 2:42: "They devoted themselves to the apostles' teaching and the fellowship, to the breaking of bread and the prayers." In Acts 6, there is a dispute that centers on food. The Hellenistic widows, those outside the Jewish community, are being neglected in the daily distribution of food. The church decided that this was important enough to appoint seven others to take charge of the food distribution to ensure that all had enough to eat. These seven, the model for what are often called deacons in our contemporary churches, took care of the important work of feeding the church and were part of the success of the church. We learn that after this dispute was settled, "The word of God continued to increase, and the number of the disciples multiplied greatly in Jerusalem, and a great many of the priests became obedient to the faith" (Acts 6:7, ESV). Making everyone welcome at the table meant the church grew as more people came to know the love and message of Jesus Christ. Tables that are places of welcome where everyone can eat without shame—about their nationality or their body size—are places that make known the welcoming love of God. The church is living out its calling when it is a community that cares for the needs of those in its midst, that includes the very real needs of food.

In Acts 10, Peter gets a lesson on food and welcome. Peter has just performed the miracle of bringing Dorcas back to life. He then goes to stay with Simon the tanner in the seaside town of Joppa, where the ocean breezes are certainly a welcome relief from the smells of the tanning industry. While there, Peter has a vision in which he is instructed to kill and eat a sheet full of animals that are unclean in the Jewish faith. Peter is confused about the meaning of the dream until he is called to the house of Cornelius, a gentile who fears God. Peter understands the dream now: everyone is welcome at God's table. Nobody is unclean. The gentiles, too, have a place in this new kingdom of God. The Holy Spirit is for all who believe, not just the Jews. Food is used here to illustrate a much larger and more important theme.

Our rules about food are microcosms of the way we view the world. Certainly there are valid food restrictions or needs, but so often, our food rules are about trying to keep control. We fall into a trap where we believe that if we eat organic, non-GMO, raw, cold-pressed juice, we will detox our body and maybe our life, too. We add a slice of lemon, Instagram it, and tell ourselves we are on the right path. We believe that if we set up enough rules and build walls around our mouth, our kitchens, our homes, and our countries, we will somehow be pure and holy and safe. Fat bodies are not the only bodies that get excluded when we believe our food rules make us holy. We exclude the poor, who we chastise for their cheap, unhealthful food and yet do nothing to address the food deserts in which they live. We exclude the immigrants, mocking their simple food that is foreign to us (until we decide it is the latest way to get healthy, and then we gentrify the prices until they can no longer afford what has been their staple nutrition). We exclude those with medical conditions and allergies, insisting that if they would just eat this or not eat that, then surely, they too would experience vitality and life.

If Peter had not heeded the message of his vision,

to abandon his food rules and his other exclusionary rules, I have no doubt that God still would have welcomed all into the family of God, but Peter would have missed that moment and that message.

Our call to feast does not mean that we hoard all that we have to pile our table higher. It means we make sure the entire community can join in on the feast. We see this clearly in the laws of the Israelites that mandated that the edges of the field be left for those in need. We see it in the parable of the prodigal son, who knows that even the servants have enough food to eat. In redemption: we all have enough to feast, and it hurts no one. In our modern contexts, we need to be intentional to make sure we are carrying out this same spirit of feasting.

Hunger is common. For the past two summers, I have spent a few mornings volunteering for a summer food program that provides lunches to children in the county who are on free and reduced lunch plans throughout the school year. The poverty rate in my county is well below average, but there are still a couple of hundred kids in danger of hunger here, and those are just the ones we know about. The problem is much grander on a global scale. As we discussed in the chapter on gluttony, we should pay attention to the impact our choices, including our food choices, have on others. If your church's potlucks are not reaching the hungry in your community, if hungry people don't know they can come and eat at your literal or theoretical table, then explore ways to make that happen. If our communities are enjoying the pleasures of fine food but we do not know the stories of those who struggle for even the simplest nutrition, we can expand the sources of our information and then act better when we know better. School social workers, health clinics, government offices, low-income housing areas, food banks, and local social-service facilities may be able to help point you in a direction where you can begin to address hunger in your community. Beyond your local community, you can look for ways to address global poverty and food insecurity. Numerous organizations are working on this task. I encourage you to find ones with the goal of creating and strengthening local economies, rather than organizations that simply maintain long-term gifts that must be constantly replenished. Numerous Christian groups and denominations have standing disaster response teams that you can train to be a part of to meet immediate hunger and other needs when disaster strikes.

Food is one of the primary ways we come together as a community that allow us to serve and share and get to know each other. When we welcome everyone and supply people with the nutrition they need to survive, then the focus on food as something that could make our stomachs too round is pushed to the side in favor of loving our neighbors.

Not only does eating around the table with other believers encourage true unity and discipleship, but the embodied experience of eating together is the ultimate picture of the kingdom of God. It's not just about a place for everyone to sit; it's a place for everyone to eat. Food and styles of eating differ so much across cultures, but eating together is perhaps one of the easiest ways to initiate a relationship—a relationship whose ultimate goal is to be the embodied existence of God's kingdom, on earth as it is in heaven. A church that fails to celebrate the earthly table has no business in inviting people to a heavenly banquet.

A COMMON TABLE

My first introduction to my years as a houseparent was dinner. I flew to Chicago for a full day of interviews that ended with sitting down at a long table in an old house. I was joined by a dozen others—teenage girls and women who lived together in that house and had dinner together most nights. The conversation was lively, the food simple, and the cloth napkin beside my plate frayed and thread-bare.

I knew then, sitting at that table, that I wanted the job. I wanted to sit there and pass food and hear the laughter. A few months later, I moved to Chicago and spent the next three years having dinner at that table. While all of the houseparents took turns cooking, I was in charge of the shopping and the meal rotation.

I had such idealistic dreams, many of them centered on the power of food. I love cooking things that the girls in the house called gourmet. Eventually they loved it. But I had to earn their trust. I cooked simple, common meals first. Once they trusted that my food was good, I started mixing it up. I served entrees in individual phyllo-dough cups, chopped olives for what felt like hours for a homemade salsa, blended cilantro and olive oil into a delicious green sauce.

Beyond my joy of sharing food—of offering the warmth and love that comes through that—I most loved the conversations at dinner. The dinner table or the car is the best place for people to talk—especially teenagers to adults. In a house full of twelve women, body image and food issues were present, but it was thankfully not the focus of every meal. At the table, I heard about troubles at school, projects they were working on, and their plans for the weekend. I heard about the micro-aggressions they faced every day as young women of color in a predominately white, upper-class school. I heard about their families and their home communities, their dreams for the future, who they talked to on the train on the way to school, and their protests at the weekend chore schedule. The table offers a place for conversation and for relationship. A family-style dinner at a common table doesn't have to be fancy; it just needs to be a place where people can gather.

A couple of years ago, the women from my Bible study class decided to make meals for some of the elderly, single, or sick people in our church. We all gathered together one morning and spent a few hours assembling lasagnas, kneading bread dough, and whipping together butter and garlic and herbs. Then we headed out to deliver the meals and quickly discovered we had overlooked something: the people to whom we delivered the food were grateful, but they wanted the company, too. They wanted to share a table. We were able to sit down with a single woman who would have eaten alone otherwise.

When I was preparing to move to my new job as a houseparent, I brought new cloth napkins with me, remembering the threadbare one that had sat near my plate when I interviewed. I wanted the girls to have nice things, to know they are worth napkins without holes and frayed edges. As I organized the dining room linen cabinet during one of my last weeks in the house, I pulled out one of those napkins I had brought with me. It was frayed at the edges. There was a hole in the corner, and parts of it had worn thin. I smiled as I thought of the life that napkin had lived. It had been used and washed hundreds of times in the past three years. Over the three years, we sat at the table together and experienced community countless times, frayed napkins and all. Turns out, sitting at the table was more important than what the place setting looked like.

I pray that common meals become common in our communities. I saw a photo recently of a meal shared across the border fence between the United States and Mexico. People gathered on either side and sat around a makeshift table. I assume they passed food back and forth between the narrow slots of the fence. They shared life together in that meal that acknowledged the humanity of the person across the fence and did not ignore the needs and the struggles that were so apparent by the literal dividing wall between them. Dining together in whatever our context allows us this opportunity. Sharing a meal with people from various backgrounds and with a multitude of perspectives allows us to hear and know the thoughts and struggles of our neighbors. We talk when we break bread. We share stories and jokes and fears. We get to know each other, and when we know each other, we can love each other. When someone is too preoccupied with worrying about the judgments people are making about the food on their plate or counting calories instead of listening to others, we lose so much of the beauty of a shared table.

Perhaps you can start putting this world-changing practice into action. Plan a meal with someone you don't normally eat with. It doesn't have to be someone you might call an enemy; you can just start with a neighbor. Be intentional to make the meal one that is free of shame. Don't comment on whether the food is good or bad. Don't talk about a diet or if it is a food you should or should not eat. Just eat and talk and share the moment together. Listen to the hopes and struggles of your dining companions. Find some community there, and see if perhaps God has something for you to work on at the dinner table that extends beyond the shape of your body.

NOTES

1. Leticia A. Guardiola-Sáenz, "Borderless Women and Borderless Texts: A Cultural Reading of Matthew 15:21–28," *Semeia* 78 (1997): 69–81.

10

LIVE A FAT-POSITIVE LIFE

I am clumsy. And because my body takes up space in ways other bodies don't, my clumsiness has often been a source of awkwardness, and sometimes a source of shame. I remember the first time I was okay with my own clumsiness. I was standing in line for pizza in the youth room at my church and turned around to talk to a friend. In the process, I bumped the aluminum trash can nearby, and the lid loudly clattered to the ground. I momentarily panicked at my awkwardness and the way the loud noise directed all eyes on me. I decided to try laughing at myself instead of apologizing and turning down my head in shame. So I laughed a bit, made a self-deprecating joke, replaced the trash can lid, and went on talking with my friend. I didn't get less clumsy after that. I can still manage to occasionally walk into actual walls. Sometimes I laugh at myself, sometimes I sigh at myself, and sometimes I just move on. I haven't been ashamed of my clumsiness in almost two decades, though. Learning to love and accept my body has been a longer path that has required more intentionality, but the process is similar. There is no one defining moment when I made the decision, but eventually, as I learned more about anti-fat bias and saw the beauty and dignity of other fat bodies, I began to extend that courtesy to my own body.

I am often asked how I got here—how I reached the place where I did not hate my body. For many, the idea that it is okay to be fat is radical. Getting to the point where we not only are okay with ourselves, but also believe that God is, too, is difficult. In this chapter, I share a few practices that have helped me along my journey to believing that God loves my fat body the way it is, despite conflicting messages from the culture and the church. I have no five-step plan. I have no guarantees that if you try some of these practices, you will develop a healthier relationship with your body, with God, and with others. It's my prayer that you do. One of my greatest joys is hearing from people who tell me they looked in the mirror just a little bit differently that day—that they saw a glimmer of beauty or light where once they'd just looked away in shame. People don't normally jump straight from loathing to love, but the steps in the middle where we begin to accept our bodies are important as well. On the days you are ready to move toward a healthy relationship with your fat body, here are some ideas to try:[1]

Look at yourself. Start here. In the early days of learning to love my body, I spent a good amount of time standing in front of the mirror in various states of dress. I didn't compliment myself or try to find things I loved; I just got used to my body. I did my best to quiet the negative voices, but mostly I just looked and didn't turn away. I learned to see myself, to know who I was in this most basic, visual form. We often don't even know what we look like, because we are so used to turning our eyes away. Let your body be normal to you. Let there be fewer surprises in the mirror because you just looked yesterday.

After years of learning to see myself, I'm now able to catch glimpses of myself in a mirror and think, "Beautiful!" But you don't have to get straight to seeing beauty; start with just seeing what is there.

Claim the word *fat*. I started calling myself fat in

a neutral tone. Not "plus size" or "curvy" or "fluffy" or whatever other euphemism there is—just fat. I know others prefer euphemisms, for their own fat-positive reasons. Do what works for you. Find a word that is empowering and liberating (and perhaps a little bit scary at first). Find a word that tells yourself, and maybe others, that you are okay with you. Use that word, even if you don't quite believe it is an okay word yet but want to believe it. Do not use a word that you say with cynicism or bitterness. Use one that brings you some joy or freedom, or that you think has the potential to bring that one day.

Spend time in fat-positive online spaces. Make sure that part of your time online—and interacting with others in person, too, if possible—is in a fat-positive context. Look for *fat*-positive spaces, not just body-positive ones. While I acknowledges that people of all shapes and sizes struggle with body image, many body-positive spaces co-opt messages and still offer support and encouragement only for thin or average-sized women. Thin-only spaces also tend to be spaces that center on white women. If it's not intersectional, it's not worth it.

In the early 2000s, I found an online blogging community called fatshionista, hosted on the Live-Journal platform. The blog posted many pictures every day of fat humans, mostly women, looking fabulous. I was able to see the beauty in other people, which was an important first step. In addition, the members of the group talked about the political and social realities of life in a fat body, opening my eyes to oppressions I had long believed I deserved. That blog is no longer as active as it once was, but you should get some places to start if you search for hashtags on social-media sites that have to do with fat acceptance, Health at Every Size, or body positivity. For a list of my current favorite public online spaces, see the resources in the appendix.

Know your measurements. Find a dressmaker's (flexible) measuring tape, and measure yourself. You can find one of these in the sewing section of craft stores or even places like Target. Standard versions will often stop at 60 inches, so if you wear above a woman's size 24, you may want to look for the longer version that goes up to 120 inches (often pink and available at craft stores or online). Then, by yourself or with the help of someone else, take some measurements of your body. I recommend measuring your chest/bust, waist, hips, calves, and upper arms. Write those measurements down.

When I first did this, I set up my camera timer and took a full-length photo of myself. I wore something I liked and smiled. Then I used a basic photo editor to add my measurements to the photo. I now knew, and had a reference of, the number of inches around my bust, waist, thighs, and upper arms. This was beneficial in a number of ways. Much of plus-size shopping is done online, because there are so few option in local stores. Now I have the power to shop for clothes that would most likely fit me, despite the sizing variations across brands. I can wear a 3X in one brand and a 6X in another. Having the knowledge of my exact measurements was empowering.

Second, in online fat-fashion communities, it is common for people to post their weight, size, and/or measurements with their photos. Knowing my measurements, I was able to spot bodies that were similar in size to me and was astounded by thinking, "She's pretty. She looks fabulous. Does that mean maybe I look okay, too?"

Share pictures of yourself. Whether you place photos of yourself in social media, a photo album from vacation, or picture frames in your home, being visible in photos says, "Dear world, here I am!" I posted my pictures online—first within the fat-positive online spaces and then more frequently on my own social-media pages. The more I posted, the more confidence I gained. I no longer make the effort to set up cameras and timers to get full-length shots, but I'm a big fan of the idea of a feminist selfie—people posting pictures of themselves that show the world their body in the way they want it to be portrayed, including bright makeup, visible double chins, laughter, unflattering poses, engagement in activity, enjoyment of food (and not just laughing over a salad), or any number of everyday life occurrences. So often, the photos we see in the media of fat people ask us to see fat as unappealing; posting our own pictures online counteracts that narrative.

Accept compliments. I slowly learned to be intentional at believing people when they tell me they find something about me attractive. I worked to learn not to brush off compliments or make a self-deprecating comment about myself in reply. I now do my best to say thank you sincerely. Whoever is saying nice things about you in your life—choose to believe them.

Stop wearing clothes you don't like. My style has shifted and changed at various times over the years, but unless it is something I have to have for a specific reason, I no longer buy anything I don't love. I wear clothes that make me feel good because they are comfortable, because they make me feel beautiful and stylish, or both. Building a wardrobe of items you enjoy wearing may be a slow shift, rather than an instantaneous change. Clothing is expensive, and extended-plus (above size 24) is not readily available in many places.

I spent a year in which I bought nothing new, including clothes. I was in a thrift store at least twice a month and would sort through the available clothes. More often than not, nothing fit me. However, by the end of the year, I was amazed at what I, as someone who wears extended-plus size, had been able to find secondhand. I found two dresses, a couple of new pairs of jeans, and a handful of tops that were both professional and casual. I still find it difficult to find business-professional wear that fits correctly, much less is comfortable. And my calves have been defying my quest for knee-high boots for a decade now. I won't always find what I want, but I can choose not to buy the top that fits but that I don't really love. For so long, I bought anything that fit, out of a scarcity mentality, assuming there simply weren't enough clothes in my size.

Go at your own pace to process this new way of thinking. After discovering fat acceptance, I needed a few years to pass before I could talk about the idea with friends or family. This is my personality type. I figure things out in my head, and then I tell people. I had a couple of friends who knew I was trying to change my way of thinking. I had my online support community. But for the most part, I stayed quiet about it. I was battling strong foes inside my own head, trying to prove I deserved dignity; I did not yet have the strength to be the go-to "fat and happy" person in my everyday community. Announce your questions and your new way of thinking when you are ready.

Experiment with attention-getting behaviors. Fat people get told not to wear bright clothing or short hair. We are discouraged from taking jobs that would make us hyper-visible (like actor or TV journalist). We are told in so many ways to hide and blend in. Try the opposite. Wear bold makeup. Dye your hair pink, and cut it short. Wear a neon crop top for your casual Saturday errands. People will see you; pay them no mind, or smile joyfully. I once walked out of my house and down the sidewalk wearing a tank-top dress and carrying a cardigan. I made it only four blocks with the summer sun on my shoulders before I donned the cover, but those were four blocks of freedom. No one screamed and rushed their children inside, away from the sight of my body.

I heartily endorse the concept of faking it until you make it. Try something a bit bold, even if you don't yet feel bold, and see what happens.

Don't celebrate weight loss. Bodies change. They gain and lose weight, hair changes color, and proportions shift. Sometimes bodies change when we are making holistically healthy choices; sometimes they change when we are sick. Sometimes they change because we're aging. Learning to accept my body as it is gave me remarkable freedom to live in ways that I used to think were reserved for thin people. I am allowed to enjoy salads. It is not ironic that I enjoy hiking. Sometimes adding things like fresh produce and physical activity into your life can mean the size of your body changes—but not always. If your body gets smaller after you added in a new habit, don't announce the weight loss. Talk about what else is going on: how much you enjoy the food, how nice it is to spend time outdoors, the way your body has gained strength or endurance.

Our cultural context makes it almost impossible to talk about weight loss in a neutral way. And certainly do not comment on another's weight loss. You do not know why or how their body shifted shape. Stories abound about persons suffering with diseases being congratulated on their smaller frame.

Those are a few practices that worked for me. You'll find others that work for you. I am still on the journey. I am more likely to roll my eyes at weight loss ads than be intrigued by them, and I have learned to spot the subtle body shaming that is everywhere in our society. I have just in the past couple of years come to truly enjoy my body—to find beauty in the way it looks, instead of just neutral acceptance. Yet there are still days when it feels like being thin would solve all my problems, when that new diet idea seems like maybe it would work, when it seems like the perks of thinness would be worth all the costs. Those days are rarer all the time, but they happen, and that's okay. Our culture is designed to make us desire thinness, and society makes life easier for thin people. We are not likely to entirely escape its well-financed pull. Give yourself grace when you battle that force.

On the days when you don't know what to try, you can borrow my mantra: "I am not too much."

I don't think it's an accident that the Great Commandment tells us to love our neighbors *as we love ourselves*. A healthy level of self-love is needed to sustain us for the work of community. We have to be able to offer a right understanding of our own body in order to rightly understand the dignity and worth of those around us.

You are made in the divine image of the Creator of the universe. You reflect that power and strength and grace and majesty. May you live into the calling to love your neighbors in a way that embraces all the ways God's image shows up on this earth.

NOTES

1. The practices and descriptions are based on a blog entry I wrote for my personal website: "How Do You Not Hate Yourself?," J. Nicole Morgan website, March 8, 2015, https://tinyurl.com/y7bybvll.

11

BE A
FAT-POSITIVE
COMMUNITY

During the Women's March on Washington on January 21, 2017, women (and some men) from across the country rallied in support of women's rights, equality, and dignity.[1] One picture[2] by photographer Kennedy Carroll that garnered much attention was of two women, Rachel Cargle and Dana Sucho—cofounders of theripple.org, holding signs in front of the US Capitol. The first woman's sign reads, "PROTECT: Black, Asian, Muslim, Latinx, Disabled, Trans, Fat, Poor, Women." The other woman's sign reads, "If you don't fight for all women you fight for no women." The first time I saw that picture, my breath caught a bit; even in secular spaces, having

215

my body included in the demand for equality and dignity is rare. To be included so specifically in a powerful image was meaningful and significant.

I want to see an intentional inclusion of fat people into spaces. I want spaces to name anti-fat bias as something they are actively working against. I want the places we gather together as communities to be more size accepting. In my hopes and dreams, one day I am not the only one in a crowd squirming at fat jokes. One day I don't have to listen to people hate their bodies with the assumption that I do, too. One day the default will be that my fat body is welcome and included and valued when I show up in a space. That reality will take some intentionality on the part of community leadership. Our world is not built for fat people by default, and our language is often problematic, even from the pulpit.

Seating is perhaps the most obvious of ways to make your community space fat accessible and friendly. Many public spaces have already done the work of making physical structures accessible to people with disabilities (providing ramps instead of steps, offering elevators and handrails, having hallways and other walking passages wide and free of obstacles, etc.). Not all fat people need these mobility accommodations, but some do. The wider spaces are always welcome. Beyond seating and physical mobility issues, there are a variety of ways in which our communities can be inaccessible to people of size. Often leadership doesn't know to look for these areas, and people either don't know they are allowed to speak up or are ashamed of their need. My hope is that by the time you've reached the end of this book, you've been given the tools and knowledge you need to know the importance of fat-accepting spaces.

In this chapter, I list some starting points and considerations to help you make your community welcoming to people of diverse body sizes. If you are in leadership and have the authority to implement these changes, I encourage you to do so! If you are a member of the community, I encourage you to be a squeaky wheel on behalf of those who may need these accommodations. Bring up these issues in the name of caring for the body of Christ and all of our neighbors. Whether you are fat or not, you have a role to play in making the world around you a fat-positive and fat-accepting space. The following actions are ways to work to make a world that has enough space for everyone.

Intentional inclusion. My assumption is typically that my fat body is not considered when people are planning events or activities. Therefore, I greatly appreciate it when people are intentional about saying that bodies of all shapes and sizes are welcome and included. The way you word this in your community will depend on a variety of factors, but you are welcome to use or modify this example, which is worded for a church:

> We welcome everybody to our church and strive to make sure each person can worship and fellowship with freedom and love in this community. If you would like to make us aware of any accommodations that would better equip you to gather in worship, fellowship, and community, including needs based on abilities, body size, access to resources, language, or any other circumstance, please let us know by contacting [person responsible] at [email and phone].

Perhaps you could place this notice somewhere in your e-newsletter, on your website, in each Sunday's bulletin, or on signs posted in various places around the common spaces where you gather.

Just as you might mention that hearing-aid devices are available so hearing-impaired individuals can better hear the sermon, mention that your space desires to make sure everyone is comfortable, safe, and included. Provide an easy way for people to contact leadership with any accessibility requests they may have. Be specific that this includes body size, as people are often ashamed to admit they need size-based accommodations. Be up-front and public with the fact that your community desires to be accessible to and inclusive of people of all sizes.

Use fat-positive (or neutral) talk. If you've sat heavy in the pews for long enough, you are likely well acquainted with fat being the go-to evidence of sin. The idea of becoming fat is often used as a deterrent for sinful behavior or an incentive toward righteous behavior. We run the race so we don't become fat; we resist temptation so we don't become fat; we have self-control so we don't become fat. Fat is evidence of sin and failure in these examples. If I had a piece of fair-trade dark chocolate with sea salt for every time I've heard or read that chocolate is a sin, I would be one happy woman. In this equation, it is never the enjoyment of chocolate that is the sin (and that alone would be a gnostic, heretical theology), but it is the believed effects of the chocolate—that is, what the chocolate will do to how much your belly curves out and away from your body. We humans know no limits to the way we sin or the ways we express our lack of self-control; find better examples. Eliminate "fat is bad" examples from your speech. You can talk about how a race is a great analogy for Christian faith without that kind of exercise

having to be about losing weight. You can talk about
the dangers of gluttony—overconsumption—without making getting fat the absolute result of that sin.

Make sure things fit. Some things have to be a certain size or strength in order to be accessible—clothing, seating, staging platforms. In regard to sanctuary
seating, pews are my favorite, and theater-style seating is my least favorite. Those chairs that hook
together to form one long immovable row exist
somewhere in the frustrating middle. With pews, I
know I have plenty of room. They are sturdy. There
is no defined space that belongs to one person; my
body can take up as much space as it needs, and the
person next to me can sit as close or as far away as
they'd like. Theater-style seating usually means arms
on all of the chairs, rarely wide enough to offer any
semblance of comfort for my wide hips. Chairs are
tricky. There are no arms, but the expanse of my
backside is rarely confined to the obvious outline of
one chair space. It's pretty easy, if somewhat uncomfortable, to use two chairs. But then the person next
to me either skips the extra space on my second chair
or also is sitting on half one chair and half the other,
making more obvious the fact that I take up more
than the allotted space for one. I'll take chairs that
hook together over theater-style seating or other
chairs with armrests any day, but put me solidly in

the column for people who appreciate traditional sanctuary furniture.

Walk the space—your church, your conference room, the space where small groups meet—and look at the seating. Are there options for people of various sizes to meet in all the spaces? This requires sturdy chairs with wide seats and without arm rests. Other people need arms on their chairs for different accessibility reasons, so include variety. Is there enough space between chairs and tables for fat people or those with mobility aids to move about? If you have the power to change the seating, change it. Otherwise, speak up! Don't wait for a fat person to express the need; make sure it's accessible regardless.

Besides furniture, a somewhat common phenomenon is community-use clothing: choir and baptismal robes, camp T-shirts, drama and theater costumes. My teenage baptism was anxiety inducing because I wasn't sure if the robe would fit. Open the closets that contain the robes or other clothing people in your congregation wear (baptismal robes, choir robes, vestments, drama costumes, etc.). Check the sizes. If there are different styles, make sure a wide size range is available in each style. Please note: a range of size up to XL or 2X is not a wide enough range.

Ask people what they need. First, a note: If you are a thin person who would like to advocate for these changes, I encourage you to seek out the counsel, advice, and opinions of fat members of your community. I realize this is a tricky conversation. Even if a thin person has new knowledge of fat acceptance, the chances are high that the average fat person might be offended if you call them fat or ask if they need accommodations based on their size. As always, it is better to have an actual relationship with a person, rather than viewing yourself as someone who can rush in and make problems go away. Do not be a Thin Savior. Reach out to individuals and/or conduct a survey of needs in the groups.

Regardless of your size, here are some ways you can determine the needs of your community:

1. Ask specific people about specific issues. Do you notice people shifting uncomfortably in their seat? Ask them if you can offer them a different chair. Is someone not wearing the same group T-shirt as everyone else? Ask if there was a T-shirt available to them. If not, work to do better next time.

2. For those you have close relationships with, bring the subject up specifically. If you are not fat and are worried about how to broach

the subject, you can say something like, "I just read a book about honoring all bodies, especially in the church. The author is a fat [or plus-size] woman and told about how she often felt excluded because of her size. I care about you and wondered if you ever feel that way. If so, I would be honored to hear about your experience."

3. Conduct an inclusion poll, and ask about *everything*. While you're excited about making your community size accepting, go ahead and figure out other areas where your community can be more intentional about welcoming people with various needs and experiences (allergies, dietary restrictions, racial injustice, mental illness, LGBTQI inclusion, chronic illnesses, etc.). You can make the survey anonymous and ask questions where respondents can answer questions like the following:

a. Can you access gathering spaces with ease? If not, what would make it easier for you to participate?

b. Can you sit through a service in the sanctuary pain-free? Can you sit in classes or other events pain-free? If no, are there accommodations we can make to our space that might enable you to participate more comfortably?

c. When we gather for communal meals, are you confident there will an abundance of food you can eat at the table? If no, what can we do to ensure that you are enthusiastically welcomed to the table?

d. If you need to use the restroom at church, are the bathrooms easily accessible to you? If not, what modifications can we make to meet this basic need for you?

e. Is there typically clothing for community-wide activities (choir robes, church play costumes, baptismal robes, T-shirts) that works for you? If not, what do you need for it to work?

f. When you are at church, are there times you feel discriminated against because of your body? If so, and if you are willing to share, please include details below.

g. Have you felt excluded from any other community activity or practice? If so, please tell us what activities and why you felt excluded.

Provide resources. If you have a resource library or other place where people can exchange materials, consider adding a few books about inclusion (like this one!). See the appendix for other ideas of resources you can make available.

Speak up. I would love to see people of faith take the lead on moving their communities toward being fat accepting. If you are thin, do not wait on fat people to ask for what they need. (However, do be sure that people who are fat, disabled, or sick have a leading voice in what an inclusive community looks like.) Advocating for yourself can be complicated in a variety of ways; the emotional toll of asking for dignity in a world where the default belief is that fat people deserve any mistreatment they get is exhausting and scary. Thin people should share that burden in appropriate ways. Again, do not rush in with answers, but actively seek to listen and learn. For those, like me, who sit heavy on the pews—whether or not you are at a place where you are ready to speak up and ask for fat accessibility in your church or other areas of your life—know that everyone, including you, has the right to fully participate in the life of the community. Perhaps you are tired of being marginalized, tired of fighting for the right to sit without pain while you listen to the sermon. Or maybe you didn't know you were marginalized, and this book has opened a door you'd rather shut again. I, too, wanted to unlearn what I had seen when I first started that journey. It's okay to let the ideas sit for a bit; you do not have to take action right away.

Every single body is loved and a part of the family of God. Most leaders will want to make sure that the members of their community feel welcome. There is a chance that making your needs known in this area will earn you your own personal sermon on the presumed need for you to be thin. However, you could be pleasantly surprised. You could introduce your leadership to a new idea. You could spark a change in how your church approaches people of size, so that your church becomes known for loving people and valuing the dignity of all humans, no matter what size T-shirts they need to order.

Let people know if they said something offensive that shames fat bodies, especially people who are teaching or preaching or leading within the church or community. Was there a fat joke in the sermon? (Again!) Begin by asking the pastor or leader what they intended to convey, and then explain why it was offensive. Hopefully, the church leadership hears this and is willing to listen and learn. So many people don't know that fat jokes are offensive. Fat people make fat jokes all the time. We are so conditioned to hate fat bodies, even if they belong to us, that the idea that someone would be offended by or take issue with a fat joke, rather than joining in on the laugh, rarely even crosses people's mind. Be the person who makes it cross their mind.

I have a friend I met in seminary who found my ideas about fat acceptance interesting but completely new. During one of the classes we had together, we had group presentations. When her group got up to present, she made a fat joke in the midst of her presentation. I saw a look of panic cross her eyes as she glanced my way, and I smiled back at her gently. I know that it is hard to retrain our brains and our mouths to speak better about our fat bodies. I knew her mistake was habit, not intentionality. A few minutes after her presentation was done, she texted me, "I'm so sorry! It was out before I knew what I was saying!" I knew she was trying to shift her own understanding of bodies and not just honor me. I let her know that catching herself immediately was a sign that she was shifting.

Speak up—even if you have to speak up multiple times. Become known as someone who will not participate in fat jokes. Others will begin to notice, and some of them will change, too.

Your body may not be beautiful by someone else's standards (or yours). It may be sick or disabled or full of pain. But the truth is, your body is made in the image of God. It is worthy of love and care and dignity. It is reasonable to expect our communities—especially communities of faith—to be places that acknowledge that truth and welcome us into life-giving community.

May we joyfully and intentionally do the work to make our spaces—our churches, classrooms, kitchens, and coffee shops—places that echo the divine endorsement that we are wonderfully made. You are enough. And you are not too much.

NOTES

1. Much of this chapter is based on a shorter article I wrote: J. Nicole Morgan, "Making Room for Fat Christians," *Fat, Catholic, & Loved* (blog), November 7, 2016, https://tinyurl.com/y8j8kotr. Modified and used here with permission.

2. Find this photo on the photographer's website in her Women's March on Washington Gallery: https://tinyurl.com/y97kapxw.

Epilogue: A Prayer of Blessing for Fat Rolls and Thunder Thighs

Creator God, I acknowledge that my body is made in your image. I am enough and not too much. I seek and hope that I will find life abundant in the body I inhabit at this moment.

I confess that I have believed the lie that a thin body is a better body and that you, God, would prefer us thin at any cost. I praise you for the way our bodies take up space in a variety of ways.

I commit today to be mindful of the ways the bodies I see around me reflect your image. I give thanks for a God who gives us purpose and meaning, no matter the size or ability of our body.

I pray for ears to hear the lies about our worth and a voice to speak truth into the world. May my life and witness make enough space for all to gather at the table.

Appendix: Resources for a Fat-Positive Life

Books

Farrell, Amy Erdman. *Fat Shame: Stigma and the Fat Body in American Culture*. New York: New York University Press, 2011.

- A particularly relevant chapter is "Fat and the Un-Civilized Body," in which Erdman details ways that fatness has been linked to the bodies of people of color and immigrants in American culture as a way to further dehumanize and demean people.

Gay, Roxane. *Hunger: A Memoir of (My) Body*. New York: Harper, 2017.

- Gay's book traces the journey of her body after trauma. She talks openly and honestly about the struggles and the pain that come with living in a fat body. This book is needed, and I strongly recommend that everyone who cares about justice for fat people read this book.

Gerber, Lynne. *Seeking the Straight and Narrow: Weight Loss and Sexual Reorientation in Evangelical America.* Chicago: University of Chicago Press, 2011.

- Gerber studies two types of programs inside churches: weight-loss programs and programs designed to turn gay people straight. Her work is insightful and illustrates some of the ways our faith is uncomfortable with bodies that fall outside the accepted norms.

Griffith, R. Marie. *Born Again Bodies: Flesh and Spirit in American Christianity.* Berkeley: University of California Press, 2004.

- This book looks at American Christianity and American body ideals and how those two ideas have interacted over the past many generations.

Isherwood, Lisa. *The Fat Jesus: Christianity and Body Image.* London: Darton, Longman & Todd, 2008.

- Isherwood's work focuses on the incarnation in regards to our bodies.

King, Sarah Withrow. *Vegangelical: How Caring for Animals Can Shape Your Faith.* Grand Rapids: Zondervan, 2016.

- So often, books on veganism use fat shame as a way to talk people into becoming vegan. King's book is absolutely free from body shame. If you're interested in learning more about the theological argument for veganism and how we can honor all of creation (including our neighbors) in some of the choices we make each day, I encourage you to pick up this book.

Stone, Rachel Marie. *Eat with Joy: Redeeming God's Gift of Food.* Downers Grove, IL: InterVarsity, 2013.

- Stone writes about many of the ways that food shows up in our lives and the ways that can be complicated. In discussing our bodies and health, Stone manages to avoid the misleading, potentially hurtful idea that there is a certain "perfect" body type.

Taylor, Barbara Brown. "The Practice of Wearing Skin." Ch. 3 in *An Altar in the World: Finding the Sacred beneath Our Feet*. New York: Harper One, 2009.

- The book is not entirely without moments of fat shame, but it comes really, really close to being body-shame free. Taylor speaks beautifully of our bodies and how our flesh is central to who God created us to be.

ARTICLES

Beck, Amanda Martinez. "Talking with Your Kids about Fat People." *Fat, Catholic, & Loved* (blog), May 5, 2017, https://tinyurl.com/yal4dyrr.

Clemmer, Don. "Dignity at Every Size." *Our Sunday Visitor*, November 13, 2016, https://tinyurl.com/y88azf66.

Hoverd, William James, and Chris G. Sibley. "Immoral Bodies: The Implicit Association between Moral Discourse and the Body." *Journal for the Scientific Study of Religion* 46, no. 3 (2007): 391–403.

McCormick, Patrick T. "How Could We Break the Lord's Bread in a Foreign Land? The Eucharist in 'Diet America.'" *Horizons* 25, no. 1 (1998): 43–57.

Morgan, J. Nicole. "Fat, Faithful, Fruitful: Bodies in the Church." Evangelicals for Social Action, April 28, 2017, https://tinyurl.com/y97qhbfz.

Smith, Joy Beth. "Fat, Single, Christian: In Church, Being Overweight and Dating Feels Like a Sin." *Washington Post*, June 27, 2016, https://tinyurl.com/y8ads9t6.

Social Media, Websites, and Podcasts

Dances with Fat. The personal blog of Ragen Chastain, one of the first fat activists I began reading. Her blog is filled with articles and information on a wide variety of topics related to fat acceptance.

- Website: danceswithfat.wordpress.com

Fat and Faithful Platforms. A podcast I cohost with Amanda Martinez Beck. We talk about faith, politics, and culture through the lens of our lives as fat, Christian women.

- Listen: Available on iTunes and wherever podcasts are found. Direct link: fat andfaithful.libsyn.com
- Facebook: Fat and Faithful
- Twitter: @fatandfaithful
- Email: fatandfaithful@gmail.com

Fat, Catholic, & Loved. A faith-and-fatness blog from size-dignity activist Amanda Martinez Beck.

- Website: amandamartinezbeck.com
- Facebook: Fat, Catholic, and Loved
- Twitter: @FatInChurch

Fat Faith. My website with blog articles and links to interviews and other work I've done.

- Website: jnicolemorgan.com
- Facebook: Fat Faith

Fat Girls Hiking. The Instagram account that inspired me to start a local hiking group. They primarily focus on their group hikes near Portland, Oregon, but they are expanding.

- Instagram: fatgirlshiking
- Facebook: Fat Girls Hiking

Unlikely Hikers. Instagram account that shares pictures of various people out enjoying nature despite not fitting the standard of who we often expect an outdoorsy person to be. The people featured include fat people, people of color, and people with physical limitations or other differences.

- Instagram: unlikelyhikers
- Facebook: Jenny Bruso & Unlikely Hikers
- Twitter: @jennybrusounlikelyhikers

IDEAS FOR GETTING APPROPRIATE MEDICAL CARE

Here are a few things I have learned to do when I am visiting medical facilities to make sure that my body receives the correct care:

- Ask if the blood pressure cuff they use to take your vitals is the correct size for your arm. Using blood pressure cuffs that are too small can cause high blood pressure readings.
- When possible, call before the appointment and ask if the office will have needed gowns or scrubs in a size that will fit you. If not, ask how they will accommodate you or if there

is a specific type of clothing you can bring from home.

- Ask them if they have ever heard of Health at Every Size and if they are comfortable treating you from a weight-neutral perspective.

For more ideas, Ragen Chastain's blog offers a printable card with questions for your doctor, suggested responses if they advise you to lose weight, and links to suggested medical resources they can read. The cards are included in the following post: "What to Say at the Doctor's Office," *Dances with Fat*, April 1, 2013, https://tinyurl.com/y734fu84.

IDEAS FOR TALKING ABOUT FATNESS WITH OTHERS

Fatness is a touchy subject to discuss. Fat people themselves differ on how they want to talk about their bodies (if at all) and what is appropriate or inappropriate to say. Always let people lead the conversation about their own bodies, and then make sure your next step is to speak with kindness. Here are a couple of ideas for each age group. This list is in no way exhaustive. Start with the assumption that all bodies are created in the image of God and worthy of dignity and respect, add kindness, and then go from there.

With Kids

- Kids will notice things on their own. They will often make comments out of curiosity, especially at a young age. If they tell you that you are fat, you can respond with a kind "I am!" With young kids, the simple act of normalizing bodies of various sizes can do wonders. If they don't see people acting with shame about their bodies, they will learn that people can be fat and (forgive the cliché) happy.
- When your kids stare or comment on the bodies of others, the teachable moment is about the appropriate time and way to ask questions, sensitivity to others, and good social skills. The reason it is inappropriate to comment on a fat person's body is not that it is fat; such comments are inappropriate because of various other social norms about privacy and politeness. We can teach kids to be polite without teaching them that the error was identifying fat.

With Youth

- When speaking to older children and teens, address the hard issues. Acknowledge that the world is set up to favor the beautiful. Let them process that. Ask them what they think about it. Ask them if they think they should resist that and how they will do so.
- Talk about structural biases. Youth are often the ones who are most in tune to working for justice. Let them know they can change the way culture sees fat bodies by working on how they see fat bodies. Encourage them to be intentional about confronting body shame where they see it.

With Adults

- Many of us make it to adulthood hating our bodies. It is common for adults to make disparaging comments about our own bodies in front of others or to comment on the calorie count of whatever food we are eating. Make it a discipline to not make those comments. If others make those comments, do your best either to not engage or to respond with something like "I don't count calories. I give my body the fuel it needs."

- Chapter 10 focused on tips for learning to love your own body. Sometimes, though, you are trying to help others live their own life with a better body image. When people make disparaging remarks about their own body in front of you, you can respond in a variety of ways, depending on your relationship. You can try a direct statement like "Believing that you are worth less is a lie. I know it's a hard belief to change, and I am here to listen if you'd like to talk." This is not something you can fix for another person. You can seek to affirm the other person in a variety of ways, refuse to participate in body shaming yourself, and show them that you enjoy spending time with them, no matter their body's size, shape, or ability. But this is a personal journey. You won't fix it for them.

ACKNOWLEDGMENTS

I am sitting at a table at a local sandwich shop that has become a standard writing place for me this past year. The seats are comfortable (and wide!), the Wi-Fi is great, and the electrical outlets abound. Today, as I am working on finishing up a few details of the book, I accidentally ordered two meals. It is fall here, or at least we are pretending it is. I wore a jacket because the calendar says it is time, even though the weather has not yet acquiesced. I ordered soup in a bread bowl, one of those hearty meals that just says fall to me. I also ordered what I thought was a half-size salad. I was going for a pick-two option. When the meal got here, I had a ginormous bread bowl overflowing with soup and a full-size salad. The server found space on my small table in between my laptop and scattered papers and multicolored pens and highlighters. He gave me a thumbs-up and said, "Lots of food for energy to work!" I must say, jokes about a fat lady writing a fat book ran through my head, and I smiled a bit.

This would have been shame-inducing many years ago. I would have been too embarrassed to stay seated. I would have packed up all my work and left—either taking the food with me to go or just leaving it all, depending on how embarrassed I was. Today I ate the soup and the oh-so-delicious sourdough bread bowl first. I pushed the salad to the side, where it is waiting for another hour into the day of writing work when the hunger pains come again. I am choosing to believe this is a blessing in disguise, a bit of divine orchestration to get me to stay in this seat just a bit longer than I had planned today to do this work.

As I sit here with more than enough food while I finish up the book, I am thinking of all those who helped get this book out—who showed up and provided more than enough encouragement, proofreading, funny gifs, physical spaces to write, and a genuine shared excitement about this project. I could not name everyone who offered encouragement, who asked me how it was going (even when my answer was "slowly!"), and who shared their love and excitement for this project. I want to specifically thank as many as I can, though.

To early readers of drafts, thank you for taking your time to make my work better. Anna Baker, we have been friends forever, and you have the unique ability to effectively tell me to get over myself when I worry about my ability to do this project justice. You are a big part of why this book isn't still just stuck in my head. Aimee Fritz, I am so glad to have a local writing friend! You have such a gift for asking me questions that get me to write the part of the story I am forgetting. Thank you for taking the time to serve me and this project in such a significant way. Karen Gonzalez, I love your heart and your leadership to stand up for others and I am so appreciative that you took the time to review some of my words. Amalia Jones, I knew I could depend on your honest feedback. Thank you for the gift of taking the time to read this book, discussing it with others, and letting me know where it needed some work. Katie McRoberts, thank you for lending your eye to these words. I am so glad we were able to meet halfway around the world and become such quick friends! Katie Stickney, you were one of the first people I knew who was also fat accepting. Having a friend to process with all these years has been such a blessing. You planted so many of these seeds.

Amanda Martinez Beck, it is so good to have someone else on this journey of writing and talking about fat acceptance in the church. It is thrilling, if sometimes a bit lonely, to be doing this work. I am thankful for your work and voice and podcast-producing skills. Thank you for the prayers (and especially for letting me know you were praying). I am so excited to read your book!

Thank you also to my friends from the Village Collective: Azikiwe Calhoun, Jennifer Carpenter, Emily Fiankor, Yana Lentz, and Carolyn Wasson. The year we spent as neighbors and weekly dinner companions was life changing for me and taught me that community is possible. You live affirming and welcoming lives so well.

To Teresa Presley and Lori Ransom, chapters two and three were first drafted while listening to gentle waves at a lake house, thanks to your generous hospitality. Thank you for offering me a distraction-free space to write so early in this process.

Thanks also to my family for the support—for cheering me on and for knowing me well enough to not ask too many questions as I worked on this.

I am thankful to the staff and classmates at Palmer Theological Seminary of Eastern University who encouraged me to keep writing and reading on this topic, who told me my voice was needed, and whose feedback on my papers helped me refine and enhance my arguments.

Thank you to Evangelicals for Social Action (specifically, Sarah Withrow King and Kristyn Komarnicki) for enthusiastically affirming that this topic needs to be addressed and for being the first to publish my writing on fat acceptance in the church.

Thanks to Kate Shellnutt for responding to my snarky tweet and asking me to write an article for *Christianity Today*. That opened up so many doors for me to talk and write about Christian fat acceptance.

Thank you to my editor at Fortress Press, Lisa Kloskin. Thank you for seeing the dream of a book on this topic and trusting me to write it. Thank you for pushing back on words that aren't needed and encouraging me to go further. I am so proud of this book, and I can confidently say it wouldn't exist without you! I am also grateful for the work of others at Fortress Press. I feel such deep gratitude to all who put such effort into the task of making this book as excellent as it can be. Thank you Layne, Karen, Katie, and others whose names I do not know.

For the people in my community who show up, open doors, and make space for me, my voice, and my wide hips: thank you.